KIDS IN CRISIS

KIDS IN CRISIS

a workable plan for

successful parenting

ROSS WRIGHT

WITH DEAN MERRILL

B&H
PUBLISHING GROUP

Nashville, Tennessee

ISBN: 978-0-8054-4399-8

Published by B&H Publishing Group,
Nashville, Tennessee

Dewey Decimal: 155.4
Subject Heading: EMOTIONALLY DISTURBED CHILDREN \
JUVENILE DELINQUENCY

Unless otherwise noted, Scripture quotations are from
the Holy Bible, New International Version,
copyright © 1973, 1978, 1984 by International Bible Society.
Other versions include: AMP, The Amplified Bible, Old Testament
copyright © 1962, 1964 by Zondervan Publishing House, used by
permission, and the New Testament © The Lockman Foundation
1954, 1958, 1987, used by permission and KJV, King James Version.

Authors are represented by the literary agency of
Mark Sweeney & Associates, Inc., 28540 Altessa Way, Suite 201,
Bonita Springs, Florida 34135

In order to safeguard the privacy of certain minors
whose stories appear in this book, their names
and other identifying details have been altered.
The essence of their experiences, however, remains accurate.

1 2 3 4 5 6 7 8   10 09 08 07

To my wife, Bridgette,
whose practicality and passion have taught me
more about raising children than
any graduate course I've ever taken
or book I've ever read.

To Alexann and Kelsey—thanks
for putting up with all Dad's theories.
Watching you blossom is one of the greatest joys of my life.

ACKNOWLEDGMENTS

Benedictus de Spinoza, the seventeenth-century Jewish-Dutch philosopher, ended his magnum opus called *The Ethics* with this sentence: "All things excellent are as difficult as they are rare." I can think of nothing more difficult than raising children. And yet it can be one of life's rare joys.

The same might be said of writing a book. It is painful and exhilarating all at the same time. The longer you work at it, the more you realize that other people are assisting you toward the finish line. This book would not have happened without the help of the following individuals in my life:

- My father, **Dr. Jack Wright,** whose early work in behavioral psychology set a career path for me far beyond his untimely death when I was only ten.
- My mother, **Leanna Wright,** who showed me that single parenting didn't have to be a disaster. She never let me wallow in victimhood; instead, she kept pressing me with "OK, that's a problem—now what are you going to do about it?"
- My father's colleagues at the University of Colorado, **Dr. O. J. Harvey, Dr. Vince Campbell,** and **Dr. Jerry Felknor,** who were there for me after my father died and later on

schooled me as a college student in the analytic approach to behavior.

- The many **children** and **foster families** I have been privileged to serve for more than two decades.
- Finally, my collaborator, **Dean Merrill,** who caught the vision for this book, believed in it, and turned my random thoughts and stories into a manuscript of excellence.

To each of these I extend my heartfelt thanks.

CONTENTS

FOREWORD

When I met Ross Wright in the fall of 1994, he was director of a child residential treatment center, and I was a child psychiatrist. He would analyze situations, develop goals, create objectives, strategies, tactics, and logistics for every situation. Children, nevertheless, were not just abstract cases to Ross; they were real people. As a result, our clinical dogma became service oriented. Partnerships were formed to meet the mutual goals of all parties.

Ross's creative genius has been developed over the years. He now gracefully tackles the worst contentious beast ever invented by man: the foster care system. In that role, he regularly mediates between judges, hurting and abandoned children, parents of various kinds, lawyers, caseworkers, doctors (such as myself), facilities, and volunteers.

This book draws from the wealth of Ross's experience and picks up on the key feature often missing, or barely mentioned, in much parenting advice—the delicate balance between rules and relationship. It is easy for us parents to get off track in the heat of battle and lose sight of the goal. This happens whenever we do not focus on the "love bank account" (see chapter 3) even while laying down the law.

Standard parenting programs tend to tell us how to enforce rules. *Kids in Crisis* keeps the nurture of the relationship in the primary position, where it belongs.

—George F. Cresswell, M.D.
Diplomate of the American Board of Psychiatry and Neurology
Director of Child and Adolescent Psychiatry,
Cedar Springs Behavioral Health System,
Colorado Springs, Colorado

INTRODUCTION

If only . . .
If only my child would straighten up . . .
If only I could figure out what to do next . . .
If only our home could have some peace . . .

Every parent or guardian of a difficult child has a thousand wishes that begin with "if only." They think back wistfully to how they felt the day they brought this boy or girl home from the hospital. Their hearts were full of joy, their smiles were radiant, their dreams of a wondrous future were glistening. And now . . . the clouds hang low over a muddy landscape. Mothers and fathers slog on from day to day, straining against the muck, berating themselves for what miserable failures they have become.

It doesn't have to be this way.

When you finish this book, I honestly believe you will be able to say, "I've finally figured out how to have a *sense of order* in my house based on *relationship,* not just rules alone." The chaos and tension can give way to cooperation and even happiness because adult and child have gotten onto the same page.

I talk to too many parents these days who have fallen into the paradigm of a tennis match: Mom and Dad as a pair on one side of the net, grinding their teeth at one or more kids on the opposite side, and everybody gearing up to slam the ball right through the opponent's gut. The harder the overhand volley, the better. Of course, the kids are also learning more every day about how to use the racket with devastating effect.

"Get out of being the adversary," I tell these parents. "Change roles; be the referee up in the catbird seat instead. Your job is not to *beat* the young player; it's to organize the match and keep it flowing within proper boundaries." And this happens best in the context of a win-win relationship.

Josh McDowell, the famous youth speaker, is known for saying to parents, "Rules without relationship is a jail. Relationship without rules is a zoo. Relationship *with* rules is a home."

There *is* a road that leads to a home characterized by respect and harmony. It's not impossible. Welcome to the journey.

1

Kids in Major Trouble

Her shiny golden hair caught your attention at once, guiding your gaze toward her flawless complexion. Her name was Christa, and her soft blue eyes matched the sky on a warm summer day. Something about her reminded you of a pop star—could she sing? If so, she should be on stage with a band backing her up, as adoring fans screamed their delight.

Even walking down the hallway of her high school, Christa was the kind of girl who would cause a stir. Guys would pause mid sentence to take note. In her classes up through junior high, she had always done well, the high-achieving daughter of a contractor father and a nurse mother. Her grades were strong . . . that is, until recently. Dad and Mom had divorced last year, and the spark in those blue eyes now seemed a little less bright.

Mom knew the breakup was tough for her daughter, of course, and she worried about a ripple effect. She told herself she would need to keep a firm hand on the rhythms of Christa's life. In her nurselike way, she insisted that homework be done and curfews

honored. The daughter chafed under the regimen, eventually coming to a blowup. "I'm going across town to live with Dad!" she
announced, and started packing her bags.

The father, feeling guilty about the effects of the divorce, was a
classic sugar daddy, giving his little sweetheart pretty much whatever she wanted. But that didn't make for total peace, either. One
night the two of them went out to dinner. While waiting for the food
to arrive at the table, an argument flared up. Neither one of them
remembers today what the fight was about, but the words grew
increasingly nasty. Finally . . .

> Being with boys made Christa feel good
> about herself, she said. They would tell
> her how pretty she was.

"If that's the way you feel, I'm out of here!" Christa snapped,
standing up from her chair.

"Fine—go ahead," Dad replied through clenched teeth.

Christa stomped out to the car and waited. Surely her dad would
come out soon and make an apology. She waited longer. A half hour
passed, then forty-five minutes.

Inside the restaurant Dad debated whether to try to patch things
up or eat his meal alone, thereby authenticating his position. He
chose the second option. Nearly an hour later he finally paid the
bill and returned to the car. Father and daughter then drove home
in silence.

Not long afterward, Christa decided to move back in with Mom
again. As she later summarized to a counselor, "I could either stay at
Dad's house or at Mom's house—but never at *my* house. I no longer
had a place to call my own."

She did, however, find a warm welcome from the guys at school. Her knockout good looks guaranteed that. Christa's first sexual experience came at age fourteen. Being with boys made her feel good about herself, she said. They would tell her how pretty she was. They would provide her with alcohol to loosen things up. She felt closer to adulthood, more in charge of her life. She didn't need to be a slave to Mom's rules and regulations after all, did she?

Cigarettes and drugs made their entrance into her life before long, and grades began to drop precipitously. That brought more scolding from Christa's parents—but so what? She was charting her own course now. When she found herself pregnant at age fifteen, she took care of the problem herself by getting an abortion.

Mom wanted her to see a therapist. She did, and after some diagnosis, Christa was provided with an antidepressant to help her emotional balance. When she was with her friends at school, especially the guys who flocked around her, she could seem jubilant. But at the therapist's office, the anxiety would bleed through.

Finally, the weekend night came when, after some drinking with a trio of boys in a tent, she provided sex for all three of them the same night. She woke up a little disoriented, but collected her stuff and went home. When she saw the boys later that day, the conversation wasn't at all what she expected. They made jokes about her and called her a couple of rather choice names. Christa felt slammed with the sudden realization that she had been used.

She was humiliated beyond words. Her "friends" were not her friends after all. That night at home, she quivered as she twisted open her medication bottle and gulped down a huge number of pills. A few hours later, her stomach was being pumped at the community hospital.

This was the point at which the parents called the residential treatment program where I worked to say, "Help! Our daughter is really messed up—she just attempted suicide. It's not safe for her to keep going with just the outpatient counseling we've been providing. Can you get her life restarted?"

The day I first met this high school sophomore (although she was far behind in credits earned), I couldn't help thinking that here was a bright, attractive teenager from an upper-middle-class family . . . in serious trouble. How sad that the implosion of her parents' marriage had thrown her for such a loop. We would need to interrupt this whole downward spiral, call a time-out, and get reorganized.

●　●　●

At six foot four and 210 sinewy pounds, Troy cut an imposing figure as he stood in the middle of his now-empty bedroom. The walls were bare, the phone unplugged, the dresser and TV removed. Only a mattress with no sheets remained on the floor. Even the door had been taken from its hinges.

He looked around at the space that used to contain his busy, humming life as a boy. This was still his house, after all. But it certainly didn't feel like it these days.

Troy was the second of four children of a notable professor of engineering at Iowa State University. In fact, his older brother had already gone away to college, so he was now at the head of the sibling line. His father and mother held high hopes for what he would achieve; they had made no secret of their expectation that Troy would become an engineer like Dad. Education was, after all, the coin of the realm in this house. No slackers here, that was for sure.

The only trouble was, Troy could sense in his bones that he wasn't as bright as everyone assumed. School was a struggle for him. His IQ was nowhere near that of his father or his brother and sisters.

He stood about as much chance of becoming an engineer as flying to Saturn.

High school graduation was now less than two years away. Everyone would be pressuring him to send out college applications. Dad and Mom couldn't wait to tell their friends where their next son would be enrolling. The very thought of what lay ahead tied a knot in Troy's stomach.

For the last year, his attendance record at the local high school had become more and more spotty. He had found some guys who were quite willing to let him just be himself. No pressure to perform. Just hang out, drink beer, and have fun.

He began growing a scraggly beard, which didn't exactly please his mom. His hair became long and greasy on his neck. Periodic reports from school documented the sliding attention to all things academic. "Son, these grades are pathetic!" his father ranted. "What's the matter with you anyway? We're not going to have this kind of thing in this family, that's for sure. You're grounded for a month . . ."

Troy began to be more sullen, more removed from family life. Sometimes he seemed depressed. But then at other times, he would rage at his parents. They couldn't figure him out. They brought him to a psychiatrist at the university. Various diagnoses were explored; for a time the experts thought Troy might be bipolar. Assorted medications were prescribed.

Meanwhile at home, the withdrawal of privileges and comforts kept ratcheting ever higher. His guitar was taken away. His use of the telephone was next. One by one, the furnishings of his bedroom disappeared. The last thing to go was the door, because, said Dad, "He just sits in there with the door closed and shuts us out." Over time Troy was systematically stripped down to nothing in his life.

His reaction? *I don't care. They can take whatever they want—I'm still never going to be the all-star student they dream about. I'm just going to sit here and make their lives miserable.*

In spite of the restrictions, Troy continued to get access to alcohol, thanks to his friends. The evening came when he showed up in the kitchen with a bottle of beer. "What do you think you're doing?" his mother cried. "You're not old enough to have that!"

"Oh, really?" Troy snarled back. "I'm gonna drink it right here in front of you—" and with that, he put the cap between his teeth to twist it off.

"Troy, stop it!" his father yelled as he jumped up to grab for the bottle. "Do you have any idea how much money we spent on your orthodontia to straighten those teeth? You're going to break something!"

> With a mighty shove, the young man pushed his father backward . . . crashing into a wall.

Troy kept biting down on the bottle as his father tried to wrestle it away. Back and forth they jerked. Then, with a mighty shove, the young man—now a good three inches taller than Dad—pushed him backward as he shouted, "There—have the beer bottle if you want it so bad!" The father staggered and then tripped over an end table, crashing into a wall.

Mom screamed, "I'm calling the police!" as she reached to dial 9-1-1.

Ten minutes later, the police showed up at the front door to find a set of parents humiliated but also fearful. This was no longer their little boy whom they could control. This was a grown young man who was more physically fit than either one of them. What could they do now?

The police, when called to the scene of any domestic disturbance, know better than just to talk the combatants down off the ceiling and hope everyone behaves thereafter. Troy was booked on a charge of third-degree assault. When his case came before the juvenile court judge a few weeks later, he was ordered into treatment. Soon thereafter, he showed up in my office for intake processing.

Again, let me point out that this was not a disadvantaged or minority-group family in a ghetto somewhere. This was not even a single-parent situation. This was a family of privilege and success who, nevertheless, found themselves at wits' end over a rebellious, alienated, self-destroying child.

Why It's Getting Worse

Sadly enough, I could tell hundreds of stories like the two above. People who do what I do—working to intervene and salvage troubled children and teens—are busier than ever these days. Our phones are ringing day and night with parents, guardians, police, and government agency workers seeking our assistance.

Throughout more than twenty years of youth care work, I've dealt with all races, ethnic backgrounds, religious heritages, socio-economic levels, and ages. I've seen twelve-year-olds making good money dealing drugs, nine-year-olds who already know how to shoplift, and four-year-olds who can not only dissolve their mother into tears but bite her arm or ear hard enough to draw blood. If anything, it is getting worse, not better.

One state (Wyoming) found in 2003 that more than 30 percent of high school students said they had felt "so sad or hopeless almost every day for two weeks or more in a row that I stopped doing some usual activities." That figure was up from 23 percent just four years previous.[1]

According to the Alan Guttmacher Institute's research, six out of ten girls who had sex before age fifteen said it was *involuntary*.[2] The same report showed that one out of four sexually active teens gets an STD every year.

One out of three high school students report they've been in a physical fight in the past year. One out of eight had to get medical attention for their injuries.[3]

Meanwhile, millions of other homes are struggling with issues perhaps not as dramatic as the stories I've told to start this book. But even these parents lie awake at night tormenting themselves with worry. *What am I going to do with this child?* The preschooler who doesn't get invited to birthday parties because he's too aggressive . . . the third-grader who still wets the bed—even these kinds of kids can push parents to the brink. It seems that raising children is getting harder all the time.

I sometimes ask myself why. What is it about the state of the American family that is causing such heartache and stress for parents and children alike? Why do we have increasing levels of kids out of control?

My main answer will not necessarily surprise you. We are reaping the effects of an absence of structure in the way we live and raise kids. The "common assumptions" of what families do together, how they function, what kids are permitted to do and not do, what the consequences should be . . . are no longer common among our population. The concept, for example, of getting married first and *then* having sex is largely gone. (Watch any TV sitcom if you doubt my word.) Whereas forty years ago it was considered appalling to show up at a hospital maternity ward as an unwed mother-to-be, today this is normalized. The idea that teachers are to be respected and obeyed has now been replaced with heated protests to the school board any time Junior gets upset.

Kids pick up on the new climate. They notice the current advertising slogan of a certain steak house chain: "No Rules. Just Right" (whatever "right" means to you). *Why not smoke a joint if I want to?* they say to themselves. *Why not have sex if I feel like it? Why not tell my mother to go to —?* We are fast building a society with no boundaries.

> What is it about the state of the American family that is causing such heartache and stress for parents and children alike?

Some people, of course, would declare this to be a good thing in the long run. The olden days were too uptight, they say. Now we don't have to wear suits to the office. We don't have to stay in marriages that drive us crazy. We don't have to say "yes, sir" or "yes, ma'am" to the school principal or the police officer. We're, like, free to be ourselves, you know?

But along the way children have lost structure; they've lost guidance; they've lost a set of expectations that were valuable to follow. If they want to trash the school cafeteria some night, so what? If they want to call somebody an insulting or vulgar name, they'll probably get a laugh from their friends, which makes it all worthwhile, right? After all, adults do the same thing.

My older daughter, Alexann, was the head cheerleader her senior year at our local high school, one of the most prestigious in the city. The hockey team had an impressive array of talent, and as the season moved along, they overwhelmed competitors right and left. By the time of the state finals, the student body was stoked with high hopes.

The players themselves had a special motivation this particular season. The day before hockey tryouts in the fall, a popular young student named Brandon had gotten drunk at a party, gone out to his car, and wrapped it around a tree, killing himself. The stunned hockey team had dedicated their season to this young man, putting his initials on their helmets, wearing green bracelets that carried his name, and chanting his name at the start of every game. The boy's parents even started a foundation to combat teen drinking.

Now at the final game of the state tournament, facing a favored and undefeated opponent, our school fought tenaciously and won the championship in a shutout, 2-0. Off came the bracelets to be waved in the air. The joyous team captains hoisted the trophy and then skated over to give it to Brandon's father in the first row, while cameras flashed.

A few days later, Alex headed to a spacious home in our neighborhood for the team's victory celebration. Cars were already filling the driveway when she arrived. She walked in, and her mouth dropped in shock. Alcohol was flowing freely for this crowd of fifteen-, sixteen- and seventeen-year-olds. Players were well on their way to getting ripped.

I cannot believe the hypocrisy of this, she said to herself as she looked around the room. A whole season to remember the lesson of a guy who killed himself by driving while under the influence—and now everybody was getting ready to repeat his tragic mistake.

My daughter (OK, this is where I get to be a proud papa) turned on her heel and walked back out the door to head home. A couple of blocks down the street, she saw police cars coming the other direction, headed for the party. The mother in charge of the event ended up facing several felonies.

How are young people in our society supposed to figure out right from wrong, wise from foolish, reasonable from crazy, even legal from illegal when the adults in their lives don't seem to have a clue? It creates an enormous uncertainty for kids growing up. We have torn down the societal structures that guided the young toward a responsible future. We have lived as if restraint was unimportant. Everywhere our kids look, they see grown-ups "doing their own thing." No wonder they attempt to do likewise.

Forty percent of American children—two out of five—will live with their mom and her boyfriend before the age of sixteen. Every week of the year at the foster placement agency I now direct, we are picking up the broken pieces of kids whose parents are on methamphetamines, living in their car, or headed off to prison. At the time of this writing, 580,000 American kids are in formal, state-funded foster care—and that number is growing by 20,000 per year.

Meanwhile, we estimate that *three times that many* kids are in informal "kinship care," which means something has happened in the original family to cause them now to be raised by a grandmother, an aunt, an older brother, or some other shirttail relative. Granted, some of these home situations are good and stable. The kinship caregivers deserve our thanks. But others are shaky at best, and downright dangerous at worst, for the next generation.

No Quick Fix

What does it take to repair the damage? When a young person is already headed down a destructive path, for whatever cause, what do we do to turn them around? What are the signs to notice? Which tactics will work, and which ones won't?

That is what this book is all about.

It is my observation that parents in the beginning are usually slow to recognize the problem. They live in denial for months or even a couple of years. "He's really a good kid," they tell themselves. "He's just going through a phase. He'll grow out of it."

This usually lasts until *an outside voice* speaks up. When a school official, a police officer, or a youth worker gets up the nerve to say, "You know, there's a problem building up in your kid, and something has got to change," the lights finally come on. Parents may be initially embarrassed, but then they start to see what others have been seeing for some time.

Their initial response all too often, however, is to look for a quick fix. *Our family is basically OK,* they tell themselves, *except that Kelly is flunking three classes . . .* or *except that Mark got caught riding around in that car with some cocaine in it. All right—what do we do to fix this?*

In other words, they tend not to look at the bigger picture. When I start talking about the overall family system, they get impatient with me. They want a silver bullet. They want to get something that will stop their kid from doing THAT, so they can then quickly be on their way.

It's a little bit like the attitude of us homeowners on the edge of the Rocky Mountains here in Colorado. We love to build right up against the bluffs and ridges. We nestle our homes into the ponderosa pine and the aspen groves, surrounded by whitetail deer. Of course, this brings with it the risk of wildfires. We have had more than a few in recent years, including the Hayman Fire of 2002 that blackened 138,000 acres and took out 133 homes.

When the fire-prevention people come around and try to tell us that we are messing with the ecology, trying to insert our way of life into a living forest region, we don't like to hear it. When the fire department advises us to clear a thirty-foot apron around all four sides of our home, we complain that this would spoil the ambience. What we want to do instead is go down to Home Depot or Kmart and buy a handy-dandy anti-brushfire kit for $17.97 that we can put on our redwood deck and then sleep safely.

It doesn't work that way.

Neither can parents solve the problems of dry tinder that have been building up for years in the lives of their children by a quick dousing with a water hose. The tinder will just dry out again, waiting for the next spark. Any psychiatrist or counselor who tells you they can fix your problem in a one-hour session is scamming you. The entire family ecology needs to be examined. Reinforcement and punishment systems need to be analyzed and possibly rebuilt. Performance objectives will have to be set, for adults as well as children. Avenues of success will have to be laid out and paved to unleash the potential of a child who appears at first glance to have none. A whole climate of teamwork will have to be established.

At our Hope & Home agency, we teach a twelve-hour class entitled "Love to Nurture" that moves methodically through this investigation. It examines step-by-step the road to restoration and wholeness for a troubled child or teenager. In the chapters of this book, we will outline much of what this course has proven to achieve over years of use.

Sometimes it may feel as difficult as trying to bend steel. What does that require by the way? A combination of *heat, pressure,* and *time.* You don't just walk around banging the steel beam against a tree, a sidewalk, or a door frame. If you did, the only dent would be in the object, not the steel. Instead, you have to raise the temperature of the steel, then carefully bring pressure to bear upon it over a period of minutes. Only then will you achieve the reshaping of this very strong metal.

Reshaping an obstinate kid is much the same. It doesn't happen overnight. It doesn't happen by blunt force. It is instead a complex process over time.

Breaking Through

But it can be done! It's not as impossible as it looks at first. I have seen too many tough kids turned around to ever give up hope. I have seen too many parents and guardians learn fresh concepts and develop practical strategies that have changed hostility into friendship and gloom into smiles.

I will never forget a hardened fourteen-year-old named Jalisha whom the courts shipped out to our facility from the mean streets of Gary, Indiana. She was hard as nails, with a very dynamic personality. Put her in any room of kids, and within five minutes she would be running the show. Even in our residential program, she let it be known that she was creating her own "G," as she called it—her term for "gang." She knew how to make it happen from her experience back east, and she claimed she was already connected to the "G" out here. So she had the power to help people or hurt them if things didn't go her way.

The more I got to know Jalisha's story, the more I believed she was not just bluffing. The oldest of three children, she had two little brothers; they knew who their dad was but seldom saw him. Meanwhile, their hardworking mom put in long hours as a maid in a downtown hotel, which left the kids on their own. The mom had once abused drugs but now was sincerely trying to do everything she could for her offspring. She loved them deeply. Of course, the high-crime neighborhood certainly didn't help; the staccato of gunfire punctured nearly every nighttime. Trash fires in metal drums on the street corners lit up the darkness, providing warmth to those standing around drinking.

Jalisha's home not only had big wrought-iron bars on every outside door and window, but even the *interior* doors were similarly fortified. Apparently if someone broke into the apartment, the residents wanted to be able to at least retreat to a bedroom and stay safe.

Jalisha had been rushed into a gang at the age of twelve. Her entry requirements, the boys explained, were twofold: (1) submit to group sex with all the members of the gang, which numbered some fifteen; and (2) shoot somebody point-blank in a public place. Once she accomplished these two things, she would be accepted as a full-fledged member.

The shooting was set up for an outdoor concert where thousands would be milling around listening to loud music. She took the handgun they gave her and waded into the crowd. There she picked out a middle-aged man at random. She raised her weapon, fired a bullet into his chest, and instantly darted for the shadows as people screamed.

Jalisha was never caught for this act of violence, and in fact, she never knew whether the man lived or died. All she knew was that now she had crossed a line. She had entered a group she could not leave. They owned her. They were now her supervisor instead of her mother—and openly said so. The die was cast.

Two years passed, with increasing gang activity, until finally Jalisha got arrested. The court was astute enough to know that she had to get out of Gary if there was to be any hope of rescuing her future. Off to Colorado she went.

She quickly became our number one rabble-rouser. Her skill at intimidating other kids was amazing. Even some of our therapists were rattled. A couple of them gave notice that they would prefer not to work with her.

We believed, however, that the steel in this troubled young woman could be bent. We applied the Love to Nurture strategies that I will outline in future chapters. We let her know that we cared about her and would find socially acceptable ways for her to succeed. One of those channels turned out to be our student council; I placed her as a member of that group! Some people thought I was crazy, but it was part of my philosophy to *empower* rather than try to *overpower*. There would be no overpowering Jalisha—that was for sure. She was much too strong. As she sat on the student council, however, she began to have a stake in her own success.

Some six months after she arrived, the date came for a talent show. I will never forget the emotion of sitting there that evening listening to this ghetto girl stand up on stage—in a frilly *dress*, no less—and sing "Amazing Grace." My wife and I choked up at the sight, and so did Jalisha's mother, who had come all the way out from Indiana for the event, bringing the dress with her. The letter "G" now had a whole new significance in the heart of this unbelievably wounded girl who had once assumed she could never be anything pretty or clean.

She owned up to the fact that she had shot the concertgoer back in Indiana—a fact we necessarily had to report to the court. After investigation, the court ruled that Jalisha's sentence for this crime would be to receive treatment in a residential center. In other words, she should stay right where she was, with us.

By the time her county caseworker, Thad Low, came out for a visit, her heart was so softened that she cried at his leaving. "Jalisha, tell me about the tears," I said quietly after he left that day. "What are you feeling? How about writing down your thoughts on paper?"

On a piece of three-hole lined paper, she wrote:

THANKS TO YOU . . .

When it was me and my 2 brothers
All alone.
We couldn't run, we couldn't hide, we had
No home.
When it was me and my 2 brothers
We had no choice
When it was me and my 2 brothers
We had no voice.
When it was me and my 2 brothers
Cocaine took over my mother . . .

As I grew older I began to understand.
When it was me and my 2 brothers
We needed a helping hand.

So to the MAN over Lake County
Thank you for taking me in
even though I was only ten,
Thanks to you, me and my 2 brothers are fine
Thanks to you, my mother's off cocaine
Thanks to you, I'm going down the right lane.

Before she left our program at around the nine-month mark, she drew me a picture. It showed a heart ripped in two, and then on the right side of the drawing, the same heart patched back together again. When she gave it to me, she gave me a hug and said, "I don't want you to forget me. Come see me in Gary, OK?"

She returned to her home, stayed out of the gang, went back to her local high school—and graduated, which was a huge achievement. When she reached her eighteenth birthday, her case file in the county records was permanently closed. No need to track her any further.

- - -

We dare not give up on the Christas and Troys and Jalishas of this world. They are children God gave us in the first place. He meant for them to be more than dysfunctional failures in life. Our hopes for them when they were little—well, at least some of those hopes— can still come true. We are not incapable of bringing about change in their personality and behavior, even at this stage.

Let's get started.

2

You Don't Need
a Bigger Hammer

If force could solve our issues with difficult kids, we would have achieved family peace a long time ago. Yet how many times in my life have I sat across the desk or the conference table from a father, mother, and surly son (or daughter) sensing that power applications were only making matters worse?

The scene usually looks like this: Dad and Mom sit close together, fidgeting and tense. The lines in their faces are drawn tight. They may even be holding hands. Their eyes meet mine, then go to the floor, then back to any papers they may have brought along. The one direction they do *not* look is five feet away to the young person who slouches in a chair, an expression of deadness on his face. His arms are crossed. His ball cap is pulled down low on his forehead. He lets out a sigh, as if to say *Can we just get this stupid meeting over with?*

Dad begins the litany of offenses. He and his wife are past the early denials now. They freely admit (almost too vigorously) that their son is doing this, that, and the other, and it's really a problem; and they've tried to counter with this and with that, to no avail. So what do they do next?

It almost sounds like a patient in a doctor's office saying, "I started out treating this aching shoulder with Tylenol, but it didn't stop the pain. So I went up to Extra-Strength Advil, and still it kept hurting. How about some codeine?" If that doesn't do the trick, they'll soon be back asking for morphine.

They are looking for some kind of escalation to get on top of their discomfort.

Hammers People Use

Here are some of the "hammers" that parents and guardians use to modify the unpleasant behavior of their children. I am not saying these are wrong; in fact, my wife and I have used many of them at one time or another, in moderation, with our own children. But as you will see, each of them has its limitations—and its potential abuses.

Time-out. The problem child is sent to a chair, a stool, or their room for a period of isolation. This tactic certainly has its merits, of course. For one thing, it removes the "audience" to whom the child may have been playing inappropriately. It gives both parties— child and adult—a chance to cool down.

However, I've known some parents who have extended the time-out beyond all reason. A good rule of thumb is that a child can be isolated one minute for every year of their age. An eight-year-old, for example, could get an eight-minute time-out. But I've heard parents of eight-year-olds say, "Yeah, I put him in his room for four hours." That's just absurd.

Some angry adults also don't stop to remember what all is waiting to entertain the child in many of today's bedrooms. According to a Kaiser Family Foundation survey of two thousand children in grades three through twelve, a record 68 percent now have a TV in their rooms. DVD players and video game consoles are often available as well. "We have changed our children's bedrooms into little media arcades," said survey codirector Donald Roberts of Stanford University. "When I was a child, 'Go to your room' was punishment. Now it's 'Go to your room and have a ball.'"[1]

> Grounding, like any useful tactic,
> can be dreadfully overused.

Grounding. This is equally popular among today's parents, especially as children grow older. It does get their attention, to be sure. But like any useful tactic, it can be dreadfully overused. If a kid senses hostility or a perverse sense of pleasure in the adult's tone when he or she announces, "OK, you're grounded!" then resentment is sure to build.

And once again, length makes a critical difference. Being grounded for a weekend is one thing; being grounded for a whole semester, on the other hand, seems downright sadistic in the kid's mind.

Confiscation. Loss of one's stuff is a useful penalty, in moderation. To live without telephone privileges or access to the family computer, for example, can drive home a point. But when it reaches the extreme I described in Troy's case in the previous chapter, where the entire bedroom was stripped except for a bare mattress, the child feels nothing but persecution.

Chores. All kids, of course, need to help the household operation as a matter of routine. There's nothing negative about this. So when chores are added as a consequence of misbehavior, it introduces confusion to the child's mind. Does this mean that if he would be really good, he wouldn't have to do chores at all? No, that wasn't the point, we parents say. But a child might understandably draw that conclusion.

Natural consequences. Granted, we all have to experience the fruit of our actions. If a child doesn't get out of bed in time, she may miss the school bus and have to walk instead. Similar things happen in the adult world. But I'm talking rather about consequences that convey shame, as in "I don't like the way your hair looks, so we're not going to take you out to a restaurant with us. You just stay home by yourself." This kind of approach builds antagonism.

> We all run into situations sooner or later with our kids that can't be fixed by force alone.

Financial leverage. Every child knows that parents pay the bills in life. Such giving needs to be done with a positive spirit. Everything goes sour when Dad snaps, "You keep mouthing off to your mother like that, and you can forget about going to college." Talk about bringing out the howitzer to kill a gnat! A sentence such as this is a case of serious overkill.

Furthermore, the consequence is much too long-range. It carries no meaning *today*. It merely threatens that someday, far down the road, there will be a punishment.

Instead of inviting a change of verbal tone or an apology from the child, it provokes retaliation. The conflict escalates. Far better for Dad to go to the son's or daughter's bedroom and say, in a quiet voice, "Hmmm, I don't know what to do now. Your mom's out there in the kitchen crying. What do you think?" A dialogue begins, hopefully eliciting empathy for the victim.

Physical punishment. Parents in distress tell me, "I've spanked him for doing such-and-such, and I've spanked him even harder, and he still won't quit." Or, "I've washed her mouth out with soap . . . sprayed him in the face with lemon juice . . . made him sit out in the garage in the cold."

Some of these methods can get downright scary. One father's standard consequence for his daughter's misbehavior was "OK, you have to come fight with me in the living room." He would pull her down into a full-scale wrestling match on the floor. He honestly believed this had a side benefit of teaching her how to defend herself in the future.

One day he bit her nose so badly she had to be taken to the emergency room. That resulted in the Department of Child and Family Services removing this poor girl from the home.

I've known other parents who were genuinely upset with the law because "it won't let me hit him hard enough to get him to do what I want him to do." If a mark is left on the kid's bottom, the law will label the parent a child abuser, and all kinds of trouble will follow. "Boy, back in my day, you got taken out behind the woodshed, and afterward you couldn't sit down for a week! Why can't I do that now?"

These kinds of adults have a mind-set that parenting is basically an exercise in superior force. They feel a need to show who's toughest. However, we all run into situations sooner or later with our kids that can't be fixed with just a bigger hammer.

The Mystery of Discipline

All of these are various forms of what we call "adversive therapy," which is doing something that bothers the child, irritates the child, upsets the child in the hope of preventing a recurrence of the offense. The downside is that the child may still find the behavior worth continuing. The pain of an adverse experience with Dad or Mom is a price worth paying for something the child really wants to do.

At such times we can start to feel that disciplining children is like nailing Jell-o to a tree. We pound away, and the stuff only keeps squirting off in all directions. "More nails!" we holler. Or, "Somebody give me a bigger hammer!" This is fruitless.

There is more to this picture for us adults than just trying to extinguish bad behavior. I brought this out once when I spoke to a large group of mothers that meets at my church each month. I was the only male in the room with eighty women. My assigned topic was child discipline, a perennial request from speakers.

I stood up and immediately got their attention by saying, "Good morning. I'd like to start off today with a discussion question. Tell me—how do your husbands discipline you?"

Dead silence. Scowls on faces all over the room. Nobody would even dignify my question with a retort.

"No, really," I continued in a jovial manner, "when you don't make dinner on time, how do your husbands discipline you? There was something you were supposed to do, and you didn't do it, so what does he do about it?"

You could cut the tension in the room with a knife.

"Well, OK, since there's no response, let me change the question a bit. How do your *parents* discipline you today? Now that you're all adults, how do they get you to do the right things?"

More silence. People started to squirm.

"My point is this," I then said. "Discipline works only when you have total power and control. Why do we all pay our taxes? Because the IRS has total power and control. They can make our lives miserable if we don't do what we should. Why don't we drive ninety-five miles an hour on the interstate? Because the police have total power and control. They can take away our license, make us pay heavy fines, even get us thrown in jail if need be.

"So why don't your parents discipline you as a grown woman? *Because they simply can't.* You won't let them. The same goes for your husband. You have free will as to whether you'll continue to live with him and be his wife. Power and control is not his alone.

"Now let me ask you: At what point in a child's life does he or she start to exhibit free will?"

Hands started coming up at last! "Eighteen months," somebody said. "Certainly before they're two," somebody else volunteered. I could see the crowd relaxing. They started to think that maybe their guest speaker wasn't such a brute after all.

"You're right," I continued. "Every one of us has had the experience of telling a toddler, 'We're leaving for church pretty soon now, and I am going to put your shoes on.' We pick up the kid, plop him on our lap, and force the shoes onto his feet. What happens as soon as we set him down again?"

The women laughed. They'd all been there. Pint-sized kids had exercised their free will by kicking off their shoes in short order.

"We have all found out that even at this early stage, our power and control are starting to ebb. We have to think of some arrangement that elicits the child's cooperation. We can no longer just overpower them with 'my way or the highway.'

"Let me make a flamboyant statement. In a very real sense, if your child is more than two years old, *you cannot discipline him*—at least in the sense of unilaterally forcing him to do what you want. You may get the upper hand temporarily, but it won't last without some kind of relationship that the child cares about protecting. At some point the child will be big enough to fight back if he or she wants to.

"Boys eventually grow up to the size where they can say with a sneer, 'Sure, Dad—bring it on!' Girls have all kinds of ways of embarrassing the daylights out of their moms. If a parent-child connection is all about domination, about getting on top of the other person, it is doomed to tragedy."

> People, whether young or old, do not object to changing. What they really dislike, however, is *being changed.*

I began noticing nods all around the room that day. These mothers knew full well that they could never, and didn't even want to, overpower their children. They wanted instead to work toward a far better goal called *emancipation*, producing children who grow up to take control of themselves and do the right things because they want to, not because they have to.

Here is a principle: People in general, whether young or old, do not object to changing. What they really dislike, however, is *being changed.* We change ourselves all the time. We don't like other people trying to change us.

Look at the incredible accounts of the human spirit resisting external force—the Warsaw ghetto, for example. Hundreds of thousands of oppressed people throughout human history have gritted their teeth and said to dictators, "You will not crush us!" A person who does not want to be disciplined can put up incredible resistance.

Parents and guardians of tough kids especially must give up the mind-set that says, "I know what's best for you, and I'm going to make you do it whether you want to or not." They simply don't have enough power and control to guarantee that. Whenever we have a foster-parent applicant at our agency who shows evidence of being a drill sergeant who's "gonna whip these kids into shape," we quickly back away. The prospects for a good outcome are next to nil.

Empower, Don't Overpower

The alternative, however, is not what you might fear. The world will not fly to pieces for lack of a sledgehammer. Not if the child is *empowered* to accomplish something that both he and the parent want to see happen.

The truth is, for all their bluster, kids feel terribly weak and small. Even tough kids. Even tough teenagers. In fact, especially teenagers. On the inside, they sense they are puny. And so they try to make themselves bigger. They puff up like a toad, trying to present a big façade.

If, as an adult, I try to overpower them, then they feel even smaller. They're more needy, more hungry for attention than ever. If I tell myself that this kid thinks he's really hot stuff and I need to knock him down to size, I create even more desperation internally. The kid feels crushed by me. Now he's going to try to find a way to knock me down to size in return.

But if, instead, I empower him in even a modest way, he ends up feeling big enough to cope with life after all. He isn't so endangered as he thought. He just might make it to see another day, another week, another year.

Let me illustrate this dynamic by telling you about an extreme case. His name was Adrian. He was the product of incest between his mother and her father. His whole life up to this point, at age fifteen, had been a sad trail of neglect, rejection, and abandonment. Without any sense of unconditional love from his family, Adrian was continually on edge. He got in trouble at school all the time. He could be very violent if he was upset. He could launch temper tantrums that were absolutely titanic.

Yet he clung to his family because he had nothing else in life to call his own. He very much wanted to get out of our facility and go home again. On this particular day, his mother had come for a staff consultation and had said she really wasn't quite ready for him to come home yet. This was the third or fourth time in his life that this had happened. Adrian was understandably frustrated. "How come my family never gets its act together?" he snapped as he left the room.

Soon Adrian was running amok, smashing things, hitting other people, to the point that the staff had to hustle him into the "quiet room"—a place with plain white walls and no furnishings meant to calm down an agitated person. They watched through the small, double-thick window in the door.

Adrian continued to roar and slam his fists into the walls. Soon he took off his belt and started swinging it around his head like a sling, taking chunks of plaster out of the wall. Then, more ominously, he looped the belt around his neck and began pantomiming the act of strangling himself to death.

"OK, we're going to have to 'mattress' him," a staff member said. "Mattressing" is a technique for controlling violent behavior that psychiatric hospital staffs know well. Four or five strong people take hold of a mattress at the edges and then rush the person all at once, smushing him up against the wall without injuring themselves. Then they carefully reach around the sides to grab the patient's limbs, let go of the mattress, and do a full takedown.

Being one of the larger males on the staff at this facility, I had gotten called to help do this dozens of times. I knew the drill well. Now we were going to have to do it to Adrian, to keep him from harming himself.

But I just didn't want to. As we got ourselves organized outside the door, I felt sad on the inside. I knew Adrian and liked him. He was a victim in so many ways.

I was in charge of the restraining team this particular day, and so I said, "Wait a minute. I want to try something different. You guys be ready with the mattress in case my idea doesn't work. If we have to use it, we will. But I'm going to go in by myself first and do something completely paradoxical."

They looked at me like I was crazy.

With my heart pounding in my chest, I stepped inside the "quiet room" and immediately dropped to my knees, leaning back against one wall and crossing my legs in front of me. Not that I was stupid; I was calculating how close the door was and how far the swinging belt buckle could reach. But I deliberately made myself lower than Adrian. I sat there motionless for a moment.

"Hey, Adrian . . ." I said in a low voice. "Wanna talk about it?"

I held my breath.

He stared at me, confused. He knew he could hit me. He could aim the belt right for my head. But what was this all about? He couldn't figure me out. Why wasn't he getting "mattressed" again like the last time?

Part of him wanted the aggression. He had almost been looking forward to the fight. But now . . . what should he do? There was nobody to struggle with.

He hesitated for a moment longer, then nodded his head at my question. Dropping the belt, he slumped down beside me on the floor. He started crying. Soon he was pouring out his feelings about "what a sucky life" he had. We had a long talk right there while the staff members watched wide-eyed through the window.

What Adrian needed that day was not to be overshadowed or overpowered. He needed somebody approachable to whom he could relate without fear. He needed someone to listen to him rather than intimidate him. As the ancient proverb says, "A gentle answer turns away wrath, but a harsh word stirs up anger" (Prov. 15:1).

I've thought back to that experience many times when confronted with an aggressive child or teenager who seems to be all tough and belligerent on the outside. *But what are they feeling on the inside?* I ask myself. *What can I do to let the steam out of the pressure cooker?*

Free to Mess Up

I was driving one day with my own daughter, who is not a problem child in any sense of the word. But even she lives with issues of control and self-differentiation, like any young person. "Hey, do you know what my teacher said the other day?" she suddenly asked me. "We were talking in class about the future, and my teacher said, 'Well, just two years from now all you guys will be in college. You can drink if you want. You can do drugs if you want. You can stay out as late as you want. You can sleep with whomever you want. You'll be eighteen, and nobody can stop you.'"

I had a hard time believing that was what the teacher had actually said; I couldn't help wondering if something had been added to the translation here. But at the same time I got ready to respond like an overpowering adult: *Oh, really? Is that so? And I'm paying for college so all that can go on? Don't think so, kid! Forget it! As long as I'm footing the bill, you'll do no such thing. . . .*

I stopped myself, however, before putting my mouth into gear. I thought for a moment. Then I said quietly, "You know what, Alex?

You can do those things now. You don't have to wait till you're eighteen."

"What?!" she said.

"I'm serious. How many of your friends already act like that? You can use drugs too. You can lie to me about where you are. You can have as much sex as you want to have. You'd get away with it."

She got real quiet, then finally rolled her eyes and responded, "Dad—I hate it when you say stuff like that."

I didn't change my tune. "Well, you know you could. How come you don't?"

Another long pause. Then she answered, "Because it would make me feel really bad about myself."

"Bingo!" I shouted with a smile. "That's the goal. It's not a matter of you wanting to do something but your mean old dad won't let you. It's a matter of you owning what you've gathered over the years from Mom and me, from your experiences at church, from lots of sources. Now these are your own values on the inside."

She smiled as she kept staring out the window, deep in thought.

One day while working at the residence facility, I employed the same principle during a student council meeting. Things hadn't been going very well in this group up to that point, with kids giving me grief for every little thing. Finally I announced, "OK, as of today, we're going to have a change of moderator. Jalisha, you're in charge now. Here's the gavel."

The seventeen or so kids in the room erupted, all talking at once. "What? What? How's this supposed to work? I don't get it!"

"I'm done," I replied. "You guys are too much for me. I can't run this group anymore. Madam Chairman, what would you like to do first?"

Jalisha stared at me for a couple of seconds in shock. But soon she regained her trademark bravado and said, "All right, everybody, come to order. We're starting this meeting." She then leaned toward me to whisper, "Like, what do I do now?"

"Do you want to elect some officers?" I asked.

"Yeah, I guess," she replied. Then raising her voice, "OK, the first thing is, we're going to elect some officers." She marched them through that process, and soon they were talking about various activities they could organize for the rest of the kids.

A couple of weeks later, they came up with what they thought was a great idea. "Hey, we want to have everybody sit out on the hillside on July 4 and watch fireworks when it gets dark. OK, Mr. Wright?"

I gulped. "Let me get this straight. You want to take seventy-eight kids from all the treatment units—some of them as little as five years old—out at night in the open for an hour? How are we going to keep everybody safe? How are we going to prevent kids from just taking off?" Inside my brain, I was imagining the worst, like *How many babies are we going to conceive that night out in the bushes?*

"Oh, we'll make sure everybody stays in line," the group responded. "We'll patrol the thing with flashlights. We'll set up those traffic cone things, with tape all around the space so you're not allowed to go outside the boundary. We'll have escorts for anybody who needs to go to the bathroom." They kept outlining the safeguards they would guarantee to make this event a success.

The longer they talked, the more investment they showed. I began to see how their sense of pride and ownership just might make this work after all. We moved forward.

July 4 arrived. The entire group moved out onto the hillside that evening, they enjoyed the fireworks, and nobody got out of hand.

I'm fairly sure that some Machiavellian pressure had been applied behind my back, with student council members threatening their peers along the lines of "Don't screw this up, you understand? This is so important." But Jalisha and her friends deserve credit for organizing a successful event. They had been empowered.

The next week I asked the group, "So how do you think this was possible? How come nothing went wrong? If I had organized this evening, all kinds of stuff would have happened."

They looked at me and said, "Like, what are you, crazy? This was *ours*. Why would we wreck *our* gig?"

Everyone in life, juvenile delinquent or not, craves their fifteen minutes of fame. Everyone yearns to hear, "Way to go—that was great!" If they can't get fame for a positive reason, they will seek it negatively. They'll turn into the class clown, the class bully, the gangbanger . . . anything to achieve notice. But when they are empowered to make something good happen in their world, they readily take up the opportunity.

Nighttime Vigil

And the approval kids seek more strongly than any other is that of parents—even if parents have behaved terribly in the past. I never cease to be amazed at how embittered, arrogant, hardened, even abusive kids still want their dad and mom to notice them, to love them somehow. All kinds of ugly things may have transpired, and still they cling to the ideal of a warm and loving family, no matter how implausible it seems.

This soft spot, this hope, is waiting under the surface for us to maximize.

My mother-in-law is now in her late sixties. She was born in a tiny town in Minnesota to a fifteen-year-old mother whose husband was in the military. Two years later they had a second daughter together.

Like many teen marriages, this one was rough. When my mother-in-law was five years old, her parents split up. They didn't know what to do with the kids. They decided the dad would take the older one (her); the mom, the younger one. But then the dad received orders to report to a base in Hawaii.

So the five-year-old was dumped with a relative she didn't know while her mom and younger sister took off for California. Neither parent had enough money for a car, obviously. They both headed out of town on the train.

The little girl left behind missed them terribly. Every night she cried just thinking about them, even though they had done little to deserve her affection. *Maybe they'll miss me so much they'll come back and get me,* she told herself.

She walked with her guardian, who was a fairly distant woman, to the stores down on the main street by the train depot. On their way home one day, she silently counted how many footsteps it was back to her house. The total came to 268.

Out of this, a solemn ritual emerged. Each night when she went to bed, she would lie awake listening for the whistle of the one passenger train that stopped each twenty-four-hour period, around 10:00 p.m. As the train pulled out of the tiny town again, she would pull the covers up over her head and begin softly counting to herself: "One . . . two . . . three . . . four . . . five . . ." all the way up to 268. That would mark enough time for her mother or dad to walk from the train station. Then she would hold her breath to see if a knock would come on the front door of her house.

The knock never came.

As I listened to this heartrending account, I asked my mother-in-law, "How long did you keep counting like this?"

"Every night for eleven years," she replied. "Then when I was sixteen, I got really angry one time. I was having to find my own dress for a dance, with no mother to help me, and I just said, 'Forget it. Even if you do show up, I don't care anymore.'"

"So that was the end of listening for the train whistle?" I said.

"Oh, no—that's a different question. I stopped counting the steps at age sixteen . . . *but I still listen for the whistle to this day.* Every time I hear a train, I can't help thinking that maybe my mom or dad will still come."

I looked at my gray-haired mother-in-law with astonishment, tears filling my eyes. If only parents could fully realize what incredible power they have in their children's lives. It is stronger than the draw of the strongest electromagnet or the gravitational pull of the planets. We are their sun, and they long to be safe in our orbit.

When they begin to wobble, they need far more than a hammer blow. They need a wise and steady hand that will steer them back on track and help them catch their momentum once again. As we empower them to soar, we give them the greatest gift of all. We give them their God-intended future.

3

What Love Can—and Cannot—Accomplish

The opposite remedy from the "bigger hammer" is the well-intentioned advice to "just love 'em." Troublemaking kids are acting out because they are starved for love, it is said. If only their parents or caregivers would take them in their arms and let them know they are valued and cherished, the misbehaviors would cease. In the words of the old Hal David/Burt Bacharach song,

What the world needs now is love, sweet love,
It's the only thing that there's just too little of. . . .

I am totally in favor of loving kids—even nasty, obnoxious, rebellious kids. An unloved child is a painfully lonely, terribly vulnerable human being. While I would not go so far as to claim that love is "the *only* thing" a child needs, it is certainly near the top of the list.

As everyone knows, the words *I love you* come easier than the actions. Showing love is a tougher proposition than affirming the concept. All too often, we are prone to reason, "I love him/her, *but . . .*" Life gets complicated for every parent.

The 1999 suspense movie *The General's Daughter*, which featured John Travolta, provided a case in point. In the film, the brilliant daughter of the no-nonsense Lieutenant General "Fighting Joe" Campbell is found horribly abused after an all-night exercise, tied down to stakes on a military maneuver field. She is a West Point graduate and now a captain in psych-ops. Apparently, she has been gang-raped.

Dad comes to see his daughter in the hospital. He is concerned about her, of course; but he also thinks that if the news media makes a big deal of this, the whole effort to increase women's opportunities in the military will be harmed. It will be bad publicity. He concludes that the men who assaulted his daughter can't really be identified, anyway, and so the whole matter should be hushed up.

> If a child or teenager does not feel the warmth of love, no other tactic is going to work.

When the daughter gets out of the hospital, she goes on a self-destructive rage that culminates in her death. The Travolta character is the investigator assigned to figure out what really went on here. Yes, she was raped, but that did not kill her. The dilemma of the movie becomes, *What's worse than rape?*

A dramatic moment comes when Travolta says to the general at last, "I think I've found the person who murdered your daughter. It was you." The father is incredulous, of course. It takes him awhile to grasp that in his daughter's eyes, she was apparently not worthy of her father's rage. He had kept his emotions under cover. He had too quickly turned to the political implications of the crime. He hadn't demonstrated his love for her by going crazy. To her, this was a worse violation than being attacked by a vicious gang of men throughout the night. She lost all self-regard on that day in the hospital.

Showing love is the most powerful tool a parent has. Not just having love, and not just announcing it. *Demonstrating it* is what makes the biggest impact.

When our child comes home with a bad report card, do we love them enough to get angry about it? "Jason, I'm really upset about this because I know you can do better. You've got so much more ability than this!" It is not a fun conversation, to be sure. But it lets the child know that he matters to his parents. They believe in his value, and they're not just going to let him slide.

How many "successful" movie stars today grew up without a sense of being loved, and so their whole life is spiraling downward? No amount of money, alcohol, drugs, fancy cars, public adoration, hunky boyfriends, or bling-bling girlfriends is enough to stabilize them. They still yearn for someone's genuine love. They go careening from one escapade to the next, looking for it.

At the opposite extreme: Think about the immigrant child who arrives in America with his parents holding only a cardboard suitcase. The family has nothing. They lead miserable lives for the first years, working long hours for minimum wages. But inside this tiny apartment in a bad part of town dwells love and support. The child goes to school, learns English, works hard, gets a scholarship to college, and grows up to make an impressive contribution to society. He knows at every step of the difficult road that he is loved.

From this I draw a principle: *Love is not enough. But without love, nothing ever is.* If a child or teenager does not feel the warmth of love, no other tactic or strategy in this book, or anybody else's book, is going to work.

I have read some advocates of "tough love" who seem to say the opposite. Show your child how firm you can be, they say. Don't let kids see that they've gotten through to you. Says one best-selling author: If they run away from home, throw a party! Act like you don't care. Don't give them the satisfaction of knowing you're disappointed or worried.

Well, that is what the hard-boiled general in the movie did. His daughter's conclusion was that she really didn't matter after all. I have seen rebellious kids go out and decide to do something even more outrageous next time just to learn whether their parents truly care. They're looking for evidence of love.

I do not mean to give license here for parental tirades. There is no excuse for a forty-year-old losing control and abusing a son or daughter, verbally or otherwise. But it is entirely appropriate to show that you're deeply disappointed. You can even get emotional about it. You are not a real parent if you don't.

Love Is like a Bank Account

Inside every child is an invisible asset account that trades not in dollars or jewels or sports trophies but in love. The balance is rising or falling every day, often changing several times within an hour. At one moment, Mom smiles and gives a compliment; the love tally rises a little higher. Ten minutes later, our older brother says we're stupid or fat; the balance takes a dip. How we feel about ourselves, and therefore how we conduct ourselves in this complicated world, is directly tied to our emotional bank account.

Life at school is constantly impacting the balance. Five or six times a day a teacher says, "Here's your C." "You got a B-minus on that quiz." "Your project is late—where is it?" Everything you do is being constantly evaluated. By mid afternoon when the last bell rings, you can feel drained.

If you're a teenage girl and you open up any magazine, you know you don't look as good as the girls pictured there. You're not taking care of your skin right. You're not the right shape for the latest fashions. You need to exercise more. You're eating too much of this and not enough of that. You don't measure up.

The educational system has traditionally recognized two areas of achievement: academics and athletics. If you can't do well in one, maybe you can excel in the other. But what if you're mediocre in both? You feel hammered by the situation. Your account slides precipitously low.

And what can you do for relief? Adults have any number of things to offset their stress. They can go for a walk. They can get in their car and drive around. They can go shopping at the mall. They can call a friend on their cell phone and have a long chat. They can escape into watching a movie.

Teenagers in the middle of a school day can't do any of these. Their schedule is locked down. Leaving the campus is not allowed. Whatever stress is building up inside has almost no escape valve. If a kid bolts for some kind of opening, he will be in big trouble.

Given these realities, parents and caregivers are advised to follow three essential guidelines of "love accounting":

1. Always make deposits before you attempt withdrawals.

That is what has to happen with our checking accounts, obviously. We have to put money *in* before we start trying to take money *out*. If we don't, the check will bounce.

Putting love expressions into a child's piggy bank has to come first, before we start making demands. Everything we ask a child to do—even something as simple as setting the dinner table or taking out the garbage—is a form of withdrawal. If there is plenty of love already in the account due to our deposits, it's no problem. But if the account is depleted, the tiniest request can provoke an explosion.

Let's say you walk in the door at six o'clock from a hard day at work, and your daughter is sprawled on the couch watching television. The contents of her backpack are strewn all over the floor. A cereal bowl with leftover milk is sitting precariously on the carpet.

Everything within you wants to bark, "Allison, what's up with this mess? You know I don't allow cereal in here on the good carpet. How come your shoes are all over the place? Have you even touched your homework yet?"

Ka-ching, ka-ching, ka-ching—three immediate withdrawals from the bank account. Is there enough cash on deposit to handle this drain? Maybe so, maybe not.

Far better to make a deposit first. "Hi, Allison. Hey, you did a really great job on your hair today. I like the curl thing you got going on—how did you do that?" She will no doubt launch into a detailed description of her beautician prowess, how she saw a picture in a magazine and decided to try it out. She may even volunteer about the compliment somebody gave her in school today.

"Neat!" you respond. "That's really cool."

By now ten or fifteen seconds have passed. You've made your deposit. You then continue, "Oh, by the way, we had a talk about cereal bowls in this room, didn't we? Yeah, I thought so." You likely don't even have to mention the backpack mess because it's implied in the discussion about general tidiness. If necessary, you can always bring it up tomorrow—after making a fresh deposit, that is.

Some readers may think this is silliness or undue pampering. I assure you that, from the kid's point of view, it is not. The current state of their love account is right at the front of their mind, and any demand for withdrawal is instantly matched against the resources available. If a kid doesn't have on reserve what the demand is calling for, they're going to react.

The reaction may vary from kid to kid. With some young people I've worked with, I've seen a slump into passivity. Nobody has filled up their account in so long that they've developed a serious case of "the whatevers." Anything you ask of them elicits nothing more than a dull-eyed "Whatever. I don't know. I don't care." They've become numb. After being tossed from one household to another to another, they are pretty sure nobody cares about them. Nobody will step up to be their safety guard. Nobody will go to bat for them. If they get a fever in the middle of a school day, nobody's going to want to come pick them up. Their account is empty. Anything that comes along in life, even if it looks promising on the outside, is sure to flop.

Every year our agency sponsors a fashion show to raise awareness and money. We rent a nice facility and invite our donors to come see our kids decked out in an array of new clothes. We set up a runway, plan glamorous music, and everything. It's quite a gala occasion. I've managed to get Wal-Mart to sign on as a sponsor, donating the clothes.

I'll never forget one of our girls, Tara, who was told to go to Wal-Mart and pick out a full head-to-toe outfit she would like to model in the fashion show—shoes, purse, even a hat if she wanted. When she came back, my wife and I said excitedly, "What did you get? Open up your sack—let's see the goodies!"

All she had chosen was one black shirt and one pair of jeans.

"Is that all?" we asked. "You could have gotten anything you wanted!"

Tara's glum answer revealed that she was vaguely aware of that but didn't want to get her hopes up. If she picked out a bunch of nice clothes, something would probably go wrong and Wal-Mart would make her give them back. Her expectations had been dashed so many times in life. Why take a risk now?

This girl had gotten used to having a love account that was bankrupt. Grown-ups were not actually going to invest in her this time any more than they had in the past. That was just how life operated. Whatever.

Other kids with bankrupt accounts, on the other hand, do not sink into passivity. They deeply resent their emotional poverty, and they become dangerous. They start living to spoil things for other people (like Troy, whose story appeared in the first chapter). They've got nothing left to lose. Any mayhem they cause is at least testimony to the fact that they *still exist* and can make a stir.

They don't expect at all that this will result in positive deposits being put into their account. That would be far too optimistic. They simply want to bang their empty piggy bank close to your ear and make you listen to the clatter. If someone actually did interrupt the cycle and send a loving response their way, they would be shocked.

The principle of "deposit first, withdraw second" is vital in nurturing a healthy emotional state in young people. A wise man wrote many centuries ago, "Anxiety weighs down the heart, but a kind word cheers it up" (Prov. 12:25 *author's paraphrase*). This is true in vivid color when it comes to troubled children and youth.

2. Make many small deposits over time.

Isn't that what the financial advisors tell us all about our retirement accounts? We don't have to plunk down five thousand dollars at once. Far better to sock away just twenty dollars each paycheck. As the years go by, the accumulated sum (with interest) turns into a sizable amount. In fact, the advisors roll out impressive charts to show how modest investments that started early in our career can make us millionaires by the time our hair turns gray.

The same is true for kids' love accounts. A steady drip-drip-drip of deposits adds up to a mountain of goodwill over time. Kids start to tell themselves, *My folks think I'm really OK. They keep saying stuff and doing things all the time. I must be doing all right.*

I was explaining this in a training class for foster parents at our agency one evening when a young man in his early thirties named Charles Horton started to cry. I noticed him sniffling off to the side, and so I stopped my lecture. "What's going on, Charles?" I asked.

"I was just thinking about something my dad used to do," he answered after swallowing a couple of times.

"Would you mind telling us what it was?"

> A steady drip-drip-drip of deposits
> adds up to a mountain of
> goodwill over time.

"He was a stockbroker," Charles explained. "Every day when I got home from school, around three-thirty or so in the afternoon, he would call me from his office."

"That's interesting," I said. "How long did you talk?"

"Not very long—just three or four minutes. He'd ask me how my day went. I'd tell him what happened. Then he'd say, 'Well, I just wanted to make sure you got home all right. I'll see you in a couple of hours.' And then we'd hang up."

"How long ago was this, Charles?"

He paused for a moment to do the math, then said, "Up until seventeen years ago."

"You're talking about something seventeen years ago that lasted only three or four minutes, and still it makes you choke up today?" I asked.

"Yeah. Because that's how I knew my dad loved me. In fact . . . I need to call him tonight." By this point, the whole class was choking up. The only thing I knew to do was call for a ten-minute break.

Filling your child's love account does not require big bucks or big blocks of time. It just requires steady, recurring deposits on a small scale. The number of "transactions" is probably more important than the size of the amounts. If a child can say, "Yeah, my mom (or dad) is always coming up with something good about me," the account will never be bankrupt.

3. Start it now.

The sooner we get started, the better. Why wait? Why not get going on the deposits that will enrich the self-esteem and confidence of the children we say we love?

Our hesitation is often based on the desire to take care of an immediate problem first. "Yes, as soon as I straighten him out on such-and-such, then I'll be more in the mood to compliment him," we tell ourselves. This is plainly backwards as well as counterproductive.

If you walk into your kid's room and it is a total mess, your first instinct is to jump on him about it. *Stop! Put your hand over your mouth.* Force yourself to find something positive—anything—that you can applaud. "Hey, look at your new skateboarding poster on the wall. Did you get to go skateboarding today? How was it?"

He will no doubt respond, "Yeah, it was fun. But I really wiped out one time. My knee is killing me. . . ."

"Only one time? Sounds like you're getting better."

"Yeah, I guess so."

You've made a deposit. Now the road is clear to talk about the need for the skateboard and twenty other items to get back where they belong.

Sometimes the deposit doesn't even have to be a compliment. When a child walks into our Hope & Home office, even if I'm terribly busy, I remind myself to say, "It's great to see you! I'm so glad you're here. I was thinking about you the other day, in fact. How's life?"

At home in the evening, I will sometimes say to my daughter, "Kelsey, I'm sitting here watching TV, and I'm noticing your side view—you're really pretty, you know? I'm amazed."

She will sometimes grunt and say, "Yeah, except for this two-by-four sticking out of my face." (Both our daughters hate their noses.)

"Actually, I think your nose is beautiful," I respond. "Look at these pictures of you I took last weekend. Don't you think you look great?"

"Well, if you think so, Dad . . ."

Yes, it's corny—I know. But I've never yet met a junior-high girl who doesn't want to be told she looks good. She craves the approval. When it comes to satisfying that craving, there's no time like the present. Why delay making deposits in the love account till tomorrow when you can get an extra day's interest by acting now?

Withdrawals Are Necessary

Please do not misunderstand: Withdrawals have to occur sometimes. No child goes without the need for correction. The love account cannot be filled to the brim every hour of the week.

Connie, one of our foster moms, had her hands full a few years ago with a strong-willed sixteen-year-old girl named Ashley. This young lady was in "true love" with a boyfriend who had run away from his home situation and was being sought by the police. As soon as they found him, he'd be going to juvenile detention. In the meantime he was calling the house every few hours, wanting to talk to Ashley.

Both caseworkers—hers and his—had firmly declared there was to be no contact between the two. "But Connie, you don't get it!" Ashley would plead. "I'm the only one who understands what he's going through. He's on the edge of committing suicide—I'm serious. I *have* to help him! If I don't talk to him, he'll do something really awful, and it will be all your fault."

The foster mom, intimidated, could not bring herself to make a withdrawal from Ashley's account. She gave in, allowing a phone conversation "just this one time." No sooner was Ashley off the line than she blurted out, "We have to meet tonight! I've *got* to see him! I'm the only one who can save him. He's going to wait for me at a such-and-such a place at nine o'clock." Connie's accommodation had only dug her into a deeper hole.

That's when my phone rang. Connie outlined the crisis. She felt cornered, having compromised her position of authority. "Ross, I don't know what to do," she admitted. "How about if *you* tell Ashley she can't see the guy?" The longer we talked, the more I discovered that down deep Connie didn't fully agree with the case workers' ruling. Maybe the boy *was* suicidal. Maybe Ashley could help him. If the caseworkers found out about the first phone call, Connie knew she would be in a jam. Ashley had her over a barrel.

"Connie," I replied, "you're trying to get me to be the tough guy here so you can keep wearing the white hat. But what you've done to yourself is a phenomenon we call *leveling.* You've lowered yourself down to the teenager's level. You've given up your leadership role. And if I do what you've asked me to do, I will end up cementing you at Ashley's level.

"So I'm not going to make the speech here. You have to step up, be the parent, own your mistake, and make the withdrawal.

You need to say, 'Ashley, I messed up once by letting you talk to him on the phone. I shouldn't have done that. I won't allow that to happen again. You will *not* talk to him again or go to meet him tonight. If you do—your life on this earth as a human being will change dramatically for the worse this coming week. I'm totally serious.'"

"Like what?" Connie wanted to know.

"Like no TV, no phone use with any of her friends, no e-mail, no going out—maximum grounding. It has to be tough enough that she really doesn't want to go there."

"Ross, I can't do this!" Connie moaned.

"You have to. Whether you agree with the no-contact policy is beside the point. You have to enforce it. Admit your prior guilt, set a new course, and go forward."

We hung up. Fifteen minutes later my phone rang again. It was Connie.

"Well, I did it," she announced with a big sigh. "I told her every-thing we talked about. Now she wants to talk to you!" This was a natural outcome; Ashley wanted to appeal to a higher court, which showed that she sensed Connie's vulnerability.

"Hey, what's up?" I said when Ashley came on the line. She gave me a report of Connie's new position and then proceeded to lobby me to overturn it because her boyfriend really needed her, blah, blah, blah.

"Wow, Ashley, what else can I say?" I responded. "Connie has stated the way things are going to be. She's also said what's going to happen to you if you bolt away. Boy, I sure wouldn't want to be in your shoes under those conditions! That sounds like a really awful life for a week. Now I guess it's your decision, isn't it? You either do what Connie said, or else the roof falls in on you. You make the call."

It was hard for Connie to make her decision stick. But she hung tough. She told me later that by the next day she was feeling more confident. And Ashley had knuckled under. She had to admit that Connie wasn't being a brute; she was following the guidelines she had been given, which caring adults had crafted for Ashley's well-being. People were taking her seriously enough to do the loving thing even if it made her irate at the moment.

When Love Gets Left Behind

The lack of this kind of dynamic interchange, of love deposits continually coming into the account even as necessary withdrawals are made, is a big factor in explaining why the foster care system in America is doing so poorly. I speak as an insider, one who is spending his life trying to make it more effective. I believe we are making some headway—but we have a very long way to go.

Recently the Pew Charitable Trust did a major analysis of foster care and produced a sixty-page document stating that the system was basically broken. Likewise, the government's own audits show massive failure in all fifty states. It's hard to argue otherwise when surveys show that 30 percent of the nation's homeless adults are former foster care children. Even more shocking is the statistic that *80 percent of prison inmates* have been through the foster care system.

Why is this?

In my view, it is because foster care is essentially built on the concept of finding *houses* for needy children rather than *homes*. What's the difference? A home is a place that a child considers "mine." It is a place where I belong. A house, on the other hand, is a place where I'm simply a guest. The issue is not how many bedrooms there are, how many bathrooms, how full the pantry is, or whether there's a high-speed Internet connection. I tell prospective foster parents all the time, "The make-or-break factor in this work is *inclusion*. You will only succeed if you include this child to the point that he stops even thinking of this as 'your house' and starts using the language of 'our.'"

Face it: The world has always had orphans needing care. I don't know who took care of the tiny baby Ichabod in the eleventh century BC after his mother died while giving him birth (see 1 Sam. 4:19–22); his father had already been killed in battle that day with the Philistines, and his grandfather, Eli the priest, had just collapsed from an apparent stroke. But somebody had to step up.

Even before that, Job had told his friends, as part of his self-defense, "I rescued the poor who cried for help, and the fatherless who had none to assist him" (29:12). This was the ancient way: The community responded voluntarily to shelter and love its little ones.

As the United States grew and developed, however, the sense of community began to weaken. By the 1830s, New York City officials were openly discussing the problem of "street children"—young boys and girls who apparently had no one to care for them. The Children's Aid Society was formed in 1853 to take in these vulnerable ones, many of whom were placed on "orphan trains" headed for the western frontier, where they would quickly be put to work. At the same time orphanages began springing up in the East—more than a hundred of them by the turn of the century.

The more institutionalized the care of orphans became, the less love and attention there was to go around. Orphanage administrators soon realized they were sitting on a source of free labor. From vegetable fields to textile mills, kids were quickly exploited.

Some voices were raised against this, and a federal law was passed in 1904 to try to corral the excesses. Two years later, the Supreme Court struck it down. Reform got a lot of talk in subsequent years, but real action didn't come until the Fair Labor Standards Act of 1938, which barred child employment (except for the family business or minor chores such as babysitting or delivering newspapers) for those age thirteen and younger. (Of course, this was prompted in part by the fact that the Great Depression was raging, and many *adults* desperately wanted the jobs children had being doing.)

Then in the summer of 1965 came the momentous arrival of Social Security's Title XIX, more popularly known as Medicaid. Among its many provisions was government money for those who, if approved, would be willing to take care of extra kids in their home. Many good people stepped up to this option, people who sincerely loved children. They are still doing so today.

> You cannot legislate that people
> make regular love deposits.

But there is no denying that Medicaid moved the orphanage system from "big business" to "small business." It offered a steady income stream; you received "payment for services rendered." Many foster parents began to think of themselves in the same vein as daycare providers, only this was round-the-clock.

In my state today (Colorado), you can make somewhere around $600 to $700 per month for each child in your home—and that is *untaxed* income. If you take in, say, six foster kids, you'll be pulling around $4,000 a month, or close to $50,000 a year—which is more in the neighborhood of a $60,000 income if you had to pay taxes like everyone else. If you keep your beds full and your expenses down (in other words, don't blow a lot of your payments on clothing, toys, and activities for the kids), hey, you can do very well for yourself.

I admit I sound cynical. But I've met too many foster parents during more than twenty years in this field for whom this is nothing but business. They openly speak of it in those terms. Meanwhile, I've been present hundreds of times on moving day when kids have been switched from one house to another—and I can count on less than two hands the number who have shown up at the transfer point with more than a single black plastic garbage bag of belongings. All their earthly goods were in that one bag. Where were the toys? Where were the books? Where were the games, the backpack, the roller blades? Where was the bicycle? They didn't exist. Somehow those hundreds of government dollars paid out on their behalf every month never made it their way.

It is hard for politicians and social scientists to figure out how to fix foster care, because it is fundamentally a *program* with a *nonprogrammatic* problem. You cannot legislate that people make regular love deposits. It's like a ceramics business saying, "Let's improve our factory to make better 'homemade' pottery. Let's put in more conveyor belts; let's hire more supervisors; let's upgrade the designs." Try as they might, the product is still going to come off an impersonal assembly line.

On the other hand, how many times has a mom stayed up till two in the morning finishing off a papier-mâché volcano because her child forgot till the last minute that a science project was due? Even though she was irritated at not hearing about this earlier and the volcano had an awkward bulge on one side, Mom went without sleep because she wanted her son or daughter to feel her love. Good foster parents do the same thing. They *include* this child with all their others, and they pay a heavy price to send the message of value.

That is what love does. It has nothing to do with dollars.

Why do you think the Bible, in telling the story of Jesus at the tomb of Lazarus, includes the line "Jesus wept" (John 11:35)? Why would the Lord of the universe break down? He knew in His mind that everything was going to turn rosy in just a minute, as soon as He worked His miracle. The death of Lazarus was entirely fixable. So why the tears?

Jesus cried because He felt the family's pain. The very next verse records, "Then the Jews said, 'See how he loved him!'" (v. 36). Everyone could sense the emotional bond at that moment.

Imagine a modern father—or foster father (it doesn't matter)—coming home from work to find an eleven-year-old girl in tears because she didn't make the audition for the school play. If he logically responds, "It'll be OK, honey. There will be other tryouts in your life, I'm sure. Don't be upset about this one," she won't feel loved. She will feel isolated. But when Dad shows that he's hurt, too, it means the world to her. *He feels my pain*, she tells herself. *And I feel his love.*

In that moment, another deposit has been made.

When Love Runs Out

Occasionally I run into parents who are so distraught from the antics of their out-of-control child that they say, "I give up. I don't even love this kid anymore." They honestly believe that love has run out entirely. "Take him!" they plead. "I can't go on any longer. Everything he does is wrong, wrong, wrong. He hates me, and I just . . ." At this point, they run out of words.

What I see in this situation, as an outsider, is different. The mother would not carry that look of pain on her face if she did not still love her child. What she is really saying is this: *I'm exhausted. My store of energy is completely gone.*

Parents, you see, have their own piggy bank account. Sometimes even they go bankrupt. They reach a point where they're so angry with this child that they are tapped out.

One couple told me about the day when their guardianship of a difficult teenage girl finally came to an end. She had run away from their home at one point with a shady-looking man in his thirties, then returned a week later. She had barely scraped through her classes to get a high school diploma. Now she would be starting the next chapter of her life with dubious coping skills.

"The minute she closed the front door of our house that afternoon and was on her way," the husband said, "we both collapsed face-down into the carpet and started sobbing. Neither of us could speak for the longest time. We felt totally drained. Eventually we sat up again and just stared at each other. We'd never been through such an ordeal in our lives and hoped we never would again."

When I sit with this kind of parent who is still legally responsible for the child, I use the analogy of airplane travel. "Remember what the flight attendant says as you're getting ready to fly? 'In case of unexpected turbulence, air masks will drop automatically from the ceiling panel in front of you. Place the mask securely over your mouth and nose, and breathe normally. If you are traveling with a small child . . .' what comes next?" I ask.

"'Secure your own mask first, then take care of your child's,'" they quote back to me.

"That's exactly right. Before we do anything about your kid, we have to get a mask on you first. You're the one gasping for fresh air. Let's start with the basics." I begin asking how much sleep they are getting. I ask about food intake. I check on stimulants and prescription medicines. I ask about caffeine.

People will start admitting, "You know, I can't remember the last time I slept through the night. I can't remember the last time I had thirty minutes to myself. . . ."

It is hard to provide any kind of nurturing life to your child if you have somehow stopped nurturing yourself. You cannot make deposits into the account of a child if there's nothing left inside of you. The first need is to refuel, restore, and reenergize yourself. Then you can get back to healthy, attentive parenting of the child in your care.

happened to my Mom

Love → → → Nurture

Nurturing is, when you stop to think about it, a bigger concept than *loving*. Nurturing is what happens when you love somebody to the point of figuring out what makes them tick. You get inside where they're coming from and start to understand God's purpose in their life. You then get busy maximizing that potential.

I love plants—but I have no idea how to nurture them. I manage to kill every one that gets close to me. Meanwhile, Bridgette, my wife, has a green thumb. She reads up on what each species needs. She says things like, "This one needs to go outside for a while. But this other one needs to be a little farther from the window."

She even talks to her plants! She uses this certain high-pitched voice that she thinks plants can understand. "Oh, you're not doing so well, are you? Here, let me give you this special nutrient that I just know will be right for you." It's goofy—but it works. I've stopped teasing her about it. Now I just sit back and enjoy the wonderful green atmosphere she creates both at home and in my office. She's a nurturer.

We call our agency's training course "Love to Nurture." By that we mean that love is vital in caring for troubled kids . . . so long as it blossoms into nurture. There's a progression here. As I said at the beginning of this chapter, *love is not enough.* It is the starting point. When it evolves into full-blown nurture, it makes its greatest impact.

I will never forget a mother of two I will call Sandra. Her daughter and son were model children, beautiful and well-behaved. They each slept through the night within weeks of their birth. When they started school, they quickly rose to the gifted-and-talented program. They had great manners. They came home when they were supposed to. They followed the rules. Sandra and her husband reinforced all this positive behavior, of course. They were most proud of their children, loving them deeply.

Occasionally, Sandra would point out to her sisters about how *their* children weren't being handled correctly. She would criticize the nutritional decisions, for example. She would comment on the disciplinary shortcomings. After all, her kids were turning out so great, and it would do the parents well to follow her example in raising their cousins.

Then . . . Sandra and her husband had their third child.

The girl turned out to be an absolute hellion. She refused to nap. They couldn't take her to a restaurant because she would crawl up and over the back of the booth. Whenever they tried to set limits, she would scream. Believe it or not, she got kicked out of kindergarten—a *girl*, no less!

Suddenly Sandra wasn't so cocky about her parenting philosophy. She took her little tiger, then age seven, to a child psychiatrist. After examination, he said, "Oh, she's fine. Just a little energetic, that's all. Not to worry."

By the time the girl reached middle school, she was dabbling in drugs. One day on the schoolyard, she got into a major argument. Five girls were all yelling at once, until this girl finally shouted,

"OK, I'm going home and get a gun, and I'm going to come back and shoot all of you!"

It was in fact an idle threat; there was no gun at home to retrieve. But the outburst brought down the wrath of the school administration, which had in fact been wishing for a reason to get rid of this student. They managed to get her placed in a residential psychiatric program.

Sandra and her husband were mortified. They had been so convinced that if you just loved kids, fed them healthy food, and gave them a nice environment in a good neighborhood, everything would turn out fine. Only belatedly did they come to see the critical need of intelligent, well-crafted *nurturance* that builds upon the foundation of love.

It is to this field of learning and practice that we turn in the coming chapters.

CHAPTER

4

How a Child Develops

When an automobile comes off the assembly line, its nature is set. All the engineering is over now; it's going to run the way it stands at the moment unless a mechanic deliberately lifts the hood and makes adjustments. Otherwise, the car is what it is.

Not so with little human beings coming home from the hospital. The developmental process of the past nine months is far from finished. All kinds of skills and understandings are yet to take shape. The infant child is still a work in process.

It pays parents and guardians to understand this complex process. If they don't, they will jump to all sorts of false conclusions. "Something's gone horribly wrong with my kid!" Well, maybe so, but maybe not. The child may simply have not developed to the point of maturity that the adult was expecting. Grasping the big picture of developmental stages can shed a lot of light on the dynamics.

Three of the greatest child psychologists to give attention to this area and present their findings have been:

- Jean Piaget (1896–1980), Swiss pioneer in cognitive development
- Erik Erikson (1902–1994), Swedish-born psychoanalyst who ended up teaching at Harvard and Berkeley
- Lawrence Kohlberg (1927–1987), American follower of Piaget's work best remembered for his theory of moral reasoning

All three have valuable insights to offer. I have blended their work into an outline of my own (see chart below)—which may frustrate the dedicated disciple of any one of the three. I believe, however, that this structure fits the reality we see in children and teens today, both "normal" and distressed. It can guide us in framing responses and interventions that work.

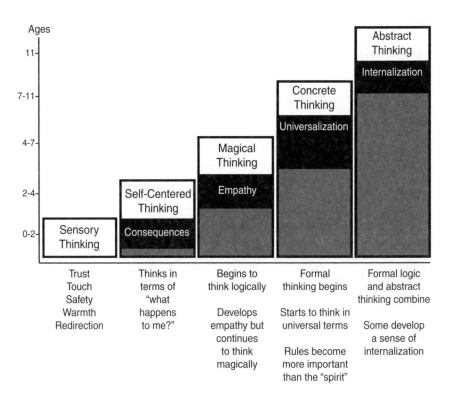

Stage 1: Sensorimotor Thinking (the first couple of years)

Infants and toddlers basically process the world through their senses—what they can touch, hear, see, taste, and smell. By grabbing, they find out that some things are soft while others are hard. They then stick the item in their mouths to see what it tastes like. They know very well when they feel dry as opposed to feeling wet. They like the first, not the second. Apple juice goes over quite well while jalapeno peppers do not.

None of these things have names yet. The baby has no language handles to attach to anything. He or she only knows what kind of sensory impression they make.

To move beyond this stage is kind of like that wonderful scene in *The Miracle Worker* when the young Helen Keller (played by Patty Duke) is a wild animal, blind and deaf, whom Annie Sullivan (Anne Bancroft) is trying to organize. She pours water on Helen's hand, then taps the sign-language code for *water* into the girl's palm, again and again. Eventually the light dawns: *water has a name! That sensation I feel—it's got something to do with this combination of finger touches. If I duplicate those finger motions, they'll know I mean* "water."

From that moment on, Helen's vocabulary starts to grow. The world opens up for her. She can process thoughts about the items in her world. She can communicate those thoughts to others. Abstract concepts represent physical things.

Prior to that day, however, she had been chained in a closed world of nameless objects. That's how it is for kids below the age of two. Because they have no building blocks, they can't create sentences any more than a cow can say, "Please milk me" or a dog can say, "I'm hot." Mommy and Daddy keep making noises with their mouths all the time, but the words themselves mean little at first.

What is especially out of reach in infancy is the "if/then" concept. "Madison, if you touch the cat's eye, then she might scratch you." Or, "Kyle, if you walk out into the street, then you will get spanked." In the sensorimotor stage of life, such combinations of words simply do not compute. The sentence is a hypothetical imperative—a most complicated declaration. It's hypothetical, in that it refers to an action that hasn't happened yet. And it follows with an imperative, a consequence that will follow the action that hasn't happened yet. Huh?

> In the sensorimotor stage of life,
> the "if/then" concept simply
> does not compute.

Consider the toddler who's with Mom in the Target store. As they enter the checkout lane, he sees the familiar colors of a candy bar wrapper. He knows his *senses* would love what's inside. So he does something entirely understandable: he grabs the candy bar and goes streaking for the exit.

The mother panics. "Stop!" she cries. Slamming her billfold into her purse, she dashes to catch up with her shoplifting son. She grabs him by the arm, scoops him up close to her face, and says in a stern Mother voice, "Michael Jeffrey Jones, where do you think you're going? You know we don't steal in our family! We have money to *pay* for things in a store!"

She is obviously saying this for the benefit of all the other watching adults, not for her toddler. She wants *them* to know that she's a good and diligent mother who's not raising some criminal here. Let the record show!

Meanwhile, Michael Jeffrey (isn't it curious how we parents drag out a child's middle name for emphasis at certain points in life?) has not the slightest concept of candy bar ownership, commercial transaction, law and justice, the significance of the line at the front door that differentiates between Target's property and personal property—all this is far over his head. He just knows Mom is upset. She barked something about not "stealing"—what's that? How does that have anything to do with the great taste of chocolate?

Next time, will he grab the candy bar again? Of course. Nothing in his realm of consciousness as a sensorimotor human being would argue otherwise. If Mom gets upset again, so what? The taste of chocolate is worth it.

The only way to discipline children at this early stage is to *redirect* their attention to some other interesting piece of sensory input— a safe toy in Mom's purse, for example, or even the red handle of the shopping cart. It also helps to plan ahead so that the off-limits items stay in the distance, beyond the reach of little hands and eyes. These actions go a lot further than a torrent of words.

2. Self-Centered Thinking (approximately age 2 ½ to 4 or 5)

By now the child is starting to build a vocabulary. Words do actually connect with things and actions. Even the notion of consequences—that Event B normally follows Event A—is beginning to take root. This works both positively and negatively. *If I eat my creamed spinach, Mommy smiles. If I squirm off the changing table, everybody gets upset.*

All such elements, however, are in orbit around ME. The child's world at this stage is 100 percent self-centered. Children assume that the Big People hold the same orientation. If Christopher comes running into the house with a skinned knee, he assumes you know he's hurt. He knows it, so automatically you should too—and should jump to his aid. Why should you have to be informed about what happened outside in the yard? He is the hub of the universe.

Piaget ran a fascinating experiment with a child this age. He set the little girl in front of a dollhouse and gave her a drawing pad and a pencil. "Draw what you see," he instructed. The girl produced a simple sketch of the front of the dollhouse.

Then Piaget took a doll and placed it on the back side of the dollhouse. He gave the girl a new piece of paper and said, "Now draw what the doll sees."

The girl produced essentially the same picture as before: the *front* of the dollhouse. That is what she herself still saw, and therefore, that's what *everybody* sees, don't they? Didn't the white-haired man in the lab coat understand that?

School therapists who are called to help after the death of a kindergartner report that the other children in the classroom are often amazingly calm about the whole thing. After all, it wasn't *them* who died. They don't really feel all that badly about the other child's mommy or daddy who lost a child. Their only apprehension, if at all, is whether such a thing might happen to them.

We adults are prone to look at this and say, "What despicable kids. Their school friend just died, and they don't even care."

No, that's just the way they're wired in the Self-Centered Thinking stage of life.

When your child spills water all over the floor and you explode with "What a mess! I just mopped this floor! How do you think this makes Mommy feel?" the true answer from the child is this: *I have absolutely no idea.* The whole concept of empathy has not yet grown inside. So you're wasting your breath. Your question has zoomed right over the child's head.

I once gave an office job to a spina bifida victim whose brain shunt had failed back when she was five. Now as an adult, she was both wheelchair-bound and blind. Her abilities were greatly limited, but we wanted to give her a chance at a bona fide job, and her family was greatly appreciative.

It soon became apparent, however, that her development had stalled back when the shunt clogged up. As a result, she had a talent for provoking her fellow workers. If she didn't like something, she would scream at people. The other staff members would say, "Susan, how do you think it makes me feel when you yell at me like that? What if the clients hear you carrying on this way?" She would look back at them blankly.

I had to pull the staff aside and say, "Guys, we can't get her to function at a level higher than she is. Our interventions need to be keyed to where she's living. Try to be patient, and I'll say to her very straightly, 'Susan, no, don't do that—it's not appropriate.' Now *that* she can understand and process."

Office life smoothed out from that point on. She simply needed a firm hand to set limits. Though I was the most direct with her of anyone, she said I was her favorite. She served on our staff for quite a while in a productive manner.

3. Magical Thinking (approximately age 4 to 7)

As you can see, there's some overlap in the time frames of these stages. No two children are alike, and no child's brain suddenly flips a switch on a given day from one stage to the next. But if you watch closely over the months, you can see the progression.

Magical thinkers are in a wonderful part of life. There really is a Santa Claus, you know! How marvelous. The Tooth Fairy really does leave a quarter under your pillow. And Harry Potter really can conquer wizards. I've known five-year-olds who said, "I made up the planet Eudora in my room—but Mom is going to make me destroy it because it's such a mess." The whole universe for kids this age is a place of thrilling enchantment. Nothing is required to be especially logical or feasible. If they can dream of something, *it exists!*

Alongside this widening view of the world is a parallel rise in empathy. Kids start to think about how others feel. It's very basic in the beginning, of course. But the self-absorption of earlier days is now starting to melt. For parents, this opens up additional methods of influencing their children. They can be brought to care about the effects of their actions.

I well remember the day our daughter Kelsey came home from school and reported, "Some kid said the dumbest thing today. He said there's no Santa Claus!"

"Hmmm," I replied. "What did you say?"

"I said, 'Well, then, who brings all the presents at Christmastime?' And he said, 'Aw, it's just your dad.'"

Kelsey rolled her eyes as she continued, "I told him, 'That's ridiculous. My dad's scared of heights—there's no way he would fly all over the world in a sleigh. Come on!'" As far as she was concerned, that settled the matter. The magical explanation of Santa Claus was a lot stronger than the Dad theory.

By the next year, however, things were starting to change. Her summer day camp class at the YMCA was planning a magic show for Friday afternoon, and my wife and I promised we'd both take off work early to come see it. On Thursday evening Kelsey seemed unusually glum. "What's wrong?" I asked.

"You don't have to come tomorrow," she said with a pout.

"Oh, I'm really looking forward to it!" I exuded. "I can't wait to see all your acts."

Her countenance grew even more sad. "Dad, I've got to tell you the truth," she said with a heavy sigh. "There's no magic. It's all just a bunch of tricks."

"Really?"

"Yeah. All the stuff we're doing—they aren't magic after all." I could tell she was totally deflated.

"Well, you know what?" I answered. "Mom and I are going to come anyway. We really want to see the tricks you guys are doing. It'll still be fun. In fact, I'm excited about the show!"

Our little princess was growing up.

4. Concrete Thinking (approximately age 7 to 11)

Soon the world becomes much more real and defined. Rules become very important. A group of grade-schoolers can blow two-thirds of their recess time simply marking off the field of play for a game of kickball. They are so into the law and making sure everything is fair that they hardly get around to playing.

They can drive parents crazy with minute inquiries. "Shelly got to stay up five minutes longer than I did. How come?!" "Don't drink and drive, Mom—you've got a soda in your hand." "My allowance is supposed to be paid on Friday but you forgot till the next morning!"

> My daughters invented a new word for people who don't stick to the rules: "illegaler."

My daughters at this stage even invented a new word for people who don't stick to the rules: "illegaler." I laughed when I first heard it, but they were entirely serious. "Dad, my sister's being an illegaler! You have to do something about it!" This concept of stepping out of bounds was entirely vivid for them and merited a swift crackdown.

One morning at our house, we had fried eggs for breakfast. The minute Bridgette put the plate in front of Alex, she said, "Why are you giving me drugs?"

"We're not! What in the world are you talking about?" I asked, baffled.

"Well, on TV, these are drugs," she blithely explained. Then it dawned on us that she had seen the classic antidrug commercial that works up to an egg sizzling in the frying pan: "This is your brain. This is drugs. This is your brain on drugs. Any questions?"

The abstract metaphor was not even close to the perspective of our Concrete Thinker at the breakfast table.

Sometimes older youth (and even adults) will revert to Concrete Thinking when it's to their advantage. I have known foster teens who, when given a curfew of 10:00 in the evening, would show up at the front door exactly on the dot, step inside, and if the foster parent didn't happen to make eye contact with them in that instant, would head back outside at 10:01 to rejoin their friends. Hey, they were "home by 10:00." Nobody had laid down any rule about what couldn't happen thereafter.

I'm sure we all remember the former President of the United States who looked us squarely in the eye and insisted, "I did not have sex with that woman." Well, technically no, but, come on. He was reverting, like some teenagers, to strict Concrete Thinking in order to conceal the full truth.

Parents and guardians of these young people have to be extremely precise in what they say. They have to work with the child for goal agreement (something we will explore more deeply in the next chapter). It is fruitless to say to a junior-higher, "I'll pick you up at the mall at 3:30." You could be chasing this kid from store to store for the next forty-five minutes in total exasperation. Instead, you say, "I'll meet you in front of the Chick-fil-A in the food court at three-thirty. Do we both have that straight? And you do have your watch, right?" Don't start the car engine until you get a clear yes.

5. Abstract Thinking (approximately age 11 through adulthood)

This stage grows into formal logic and the ability to see the grand picture. The kid can grasp that if we never take out the garbage, the house will eventually fill up with trash and become unlivable. He or she can also appreciate the role of personal reputation—if I act like a jerk, other people are going to remember that and think less of me for a long time.

Some actually reach the level of what psychologists call "internalization," the highest form of moral development. *I am a person with certain standards and values, and I'm going to stop and think about how each proposed action squares with who I truly am.* When dilemmas arise, the mature person weighs the relative values and makes an informed choice. If, for example, they have been asked to drive a bleeding person to the emergency room at two o'clock in the morning, and the light at the intersection is red but there's no cross-traffic in any direction, they will go ahead and run the red light (break the rule) in the higher interest of saving life. They are able to rank their goals in order of significance.

Some young people—and even some adults—never quite get to the stage of Abstract Thinking. Or they get there only temporarily, reverting back when stresses arise. I knew one girl who was driving her parents crazy by wandering off task at homework time. They'd insist that she sit down at the table and start cracking the books—and ten minutes later she'd be off primping in front of the bathroom mirror, doing a little channel surfing, or scratching the dog's back.

"Heather!" her mother would say, appealing to the girl's abstract thinking, "when you finish growing up, do you want to spend your life working for minimum wage somewhere? Do you—"

"Sure, Mom. I'll be a janitor. It's OK; I don't care."

"I can't believe you just said that!"

"Or I'll marry a rock star. I'll be a millionaire. You can come stay at my mansion when I'm rich." (Back to Magical Thinking.)

In such a crunch, the parent has to match the child's reversion and go back to a more straightforward consequence as in earlier days: "If you don't finish your homework, you don't go out this evening—period. Got that?" The higher level of functioning will have to wait for another occasion.

Our purpose as guides and shapers of the young is to comprehend where they are developmentally and match our interventions accordingly. If we are diligent in this, we can succeed in raising them over time to be self-regulating adults.

But we can never lose touch with where they are *today*. To give a far-fetched example: Imagine a Monopoly game being played by all the cousins after Thanksgiving dinner. The ages run from two to fifteen.

The littlest guy can't keep the playing pieces out of his mouth. He wants to know what the houses and hotels taste like.

The four-year-old thinks it should always be her turn.

The six-year-old keeps busy making the race car and the thimble fly through the air on a magic carpet.

The ten-year-old has his money all arranged in proper order and reminds everyone else to do likewise. As the game starts, he makes sure the dice are rolled only once per turn and the markers stay on the proper squares. The rules must be followed. When someone goes bankrupt, they have to leave the game.

But then the fifteen-year-old says, "Well, that wouldn't be fun. Here, I'll give Shawn a five-hundred-dollar loan."

The ten-year-old goes diving for the rule book. "No, no, no, it says right here on page 22 that 'No loans between players are permitted'!"

"Come on, Kevin, let's not spoil the experience. Let's keep the spirit of the game going, don't you think? We want to have a good time together."

Each player is coming from his or her own developmental stage. Each is acting consistently with deeply entrenched norms.

Or in a more serious vein: How do kids process the heavy blow of their parents' divorce—an event that sends tens of thousands of young people over the edge each year?

The toddler doesn't say anything, of course. But he misses that person who used to hold him closely, caress him, and kiss him good-night. He may cry more now or develop other physical symptoms.

The self-centered preschooler takes on the blame. "It's my fault. If I had been better, Daddy wouldn't have left us. I must be really bad." This child assumes he is the sole causal agent in the universe, and everything goes through his intersection.

The magical thinker may say, "Oh, but my folks will get back together again. This won't last. I'll just wish real hard, and everything will be OK."

The concrete-thinking grade-schooler is ticked off because somebody broke the rules. "You guys *promised* to be married forever. How come you're not keeping your word?" He also worries about practical things: "What will happen to our dog—does it go here or there? Are we going to have enough money? Who's going to drive me to my soccer games now that I have to be with Dad on Wednesdays?"

The more universal teenager says, "So you guys don't really love each other after all? You always tell me to stick it out. Why aren't you?" She goes to her room wondering, *Is this going to happen to me too someday? The world is royally messed up, isn't it?*

Each has a different reaction to the same outside stimulus based on his or her developmental stage. The parents, who are in the midst of their own emotional hurricane, also have a big job to manage each child's feelings. It is, as we know, a daunting task for many divorcing couples to handle all at once. Their kids spin out into dangerous waters.

The Multilayer Approach

The day-to-day world of normal family life is complex enough with one, two, three, or more kids going through the five stages on separate timetables. Parents can take heart in the knowledge that the stages *build* on top of each other. Stage 1 (sensorimotor) does not go away when the child moves into Stage 2 (self-centeredness); he's still responsive to sensorimotor stimuli. The strictly-by-the-rules ten-year-old (Stage 4) is still influenced by earlier stages as well. Once children gain an appreciation for magic, or for empathy, they never entirely lose it.

This allows the parent to frame responses that touch *all* of the preceding stages as well as the present one—in fact, the more the better. I'll give several illustrations in just a minute. But first I want to emphasize the one big mistake parents make, which is going *beyond* the child's current stage. It's OK to aim low at times, but it never works to aim high. With a self-centered child (ages 2 ½ to 4 or 5), an appeal to the Golden Rule is doomed to fail. "Look what you did to Mikey—you really upset him. You need to be willing to share." The trouble is, the meaning of "share" implies proprietary ownership, which is beyond the preschooler's grasp.

Instead, you say, "You get to play with this toy, and Mikey's going to play with that one." Then five minutes later, you say, "OK, now we're going to swap. You're going to play with the other toy while Mikey plays with . . ." The direction has to be entirely self-focused.

You can be equally direct with a Stage 3 (magical thinking) child while at the same time you can start to exploit the sensitivity to others. "You know, it really bums me out when you disobey Mommy." The five- or six-year-old can grasp this.

Dealing with "illegalers" in Stage 4 (concrete thinking) is in some ways easier because they instinctively want to stay on the right side of the law.

Finally, the Stage 5 teenager is open to far more sophistication. With all the traditions of the past, you can now add the appeal of being a person of integrity and maturity. Whenever you can elicit a response of "I don't want to do that because I'd feel badly about myself," you know you're making progress.

The multilayer approach has many applications. Think about this scenario: If someone gave you ten million dollars to design a campaign against drunk driving, what would your main messages be? How could you hit the theme on as many levels as possible?

Stage 1: Advise the public that if they have a drunk friend at their house, don't bother trying to reason with him. Don't argue; don't preach. Just take his keys, period. He has sunk to the sensorimotor level, and all you can do is what you'd do with a toddler: redirect him (to a taxi).

Stage 2: The well-known billboard says it well to the self-centered person: YOU DRINK. YOU DRIVE. YOU LOSE, meaning, you lose your license. The message has nothing to do with evoking empathy for the person you might hit on the road or making you feel guilty. It simply majors on the personal consequence.

Stage 3: Now that empathy is in play, you shoot a commercial that shows a dad and his young daughter having fun playing on the floor when—boom!—all of a sudden the dad fades from the picture. A scroll across the bottom says, "Jim Larson, father of three—killed by a drunk driver." Or you show somebody in a wheelchair for life and describe their circumstances with somber orchestral music in the background. You tug on the heartstrings.

Stage 4: Here the focus is on facts and figures. You blitz the audience with length of jail sentences for those convicted of drunk driving, the size of the fines, the career opportunities forfeited because of carrying a criminal record.

Stage 5: You play to the personal repercussions, i.e., do you really want to be the kind of person who puts others at risk? Do you want to go to parties and have people whisper behind your back, "Isn't that the guy who got the DUI awhile back?" Is this the kind of reputation you're willing to live with?

No one message will do the job alone for every citizen. It takes all of them working together to make a dent in this tragedy.

Similarly, the multilayered approach has an exponential benefit in affecting the behaviors of our children. As long as we don't get ahead of them on the stage chart, we can use a varied approach to get desired results.

Open Ears, Closed Ears

There's one more truth that makes a huge difference in our success, and it's this: *Learning is a higher function of the brain, and when any of us gets stressed or scared, we regress to lower levels of function. The more upset we are, the less we hear and the less we absorb. It's true of children, of teenagers, of adults—all of us.*

I hear parents say, "My child bolted all of a sudden out into the traffic. I ran after him, grabbed his arm, swatted him on the butt, and yelled, 'Jacob, don't you ever do that again! You're going to get yourself killed!' It's really important that he understands that."

Well . . . I doubt that little Jacob got the message. He was too scared. His mother put him in pain, reducing him to the primal level of fight or flight. His ability to learn was practically zero at that moment.

What is needed at such a moment is quick but unemotional removal from danger, followed by a period of de-escalation. The fewer words, the better, at least until everybody's pulse calms down. *Then* the parent can walk the child back to the curb for a quiet talk. "See all the cars that come down this street? That's why we have a rule in our family: We always hold hands when we cross the street. *Always.* Here, let's practice. Take my hand, and we'll go across when it's safe. . . ." But this instruction won't be effective when everyone is churned up. It has to be delivered at a later time.

> A child's greatest learning takes place when he or she is least stressed.

When your house is on fire and the firefighters arrive just as you're wondering where your kids are and which cherished items you're going to grab, they do not give you a lengthy "if-then" recitation. "Hello, Mr. Wright. It appears you have a fire here. Well, there are a couple of options. Would you like to go out the front door, which would require breaking the fairly expensive lock, or would you prefer to go out the back door, which is open but is now filling up with smoke?"

No. All the firefighters say is, "Come here—*now.* Follow us." In a stressful situation, five words is about the maximum. Later on, there will be plenty of time for talking.

A child's greatest learning takes place when he or she is least stressed. The environment is calm, not chaotic. His stomach is full. Distractions are minimal. These are the teachable moments when the brain is ready to receive. The pores of the sponge are relaxed and open, not scrunched up into a tight ball.

We parents have to read the mental state of our children before we open our mouths. If the conditions are not favorable, we need first to adjust the surroundings. We may need to reconsider our timing. What we want is a student ready to learn from us. As the old saying goes, "Communication is not what I say; it's what they hear."

Saying the right words (based on developmental stage) in the right tone of voice at the right time under the right conditions can work wonders with any child.

5

What's the Goal, Anyway?

Imagine that you're trying to sail a 2.4-meter keelboat across a choppy lake. Clouds are churning on the horizon, and the wind is picking up. Your jib is snapping in the breeze, and every so often a bigger wave hits you on the starboard side, jolting your small craft. Soon you're fairly soaked from the spray, and you're beginning to wonder if a full-scale thunderstorm is going to cut loose in the next few minutes. Can you actually keep this boat right side up, or is it eventually going to "turtle" on you?

In such a moment, it's hard to remember that you were originally heading for a famous shoreline restaurant with great steaks on the other side of the lake. You can't even see the far shore now through the pelting rain. All your attention is riveted on the immediate crisis. You're simply hanging on.

That's how it feels sometimes to be the parent or guardian of a turbulent child. A new squall seems to come your way every day—sometimes every hour. You've hardly caught your balance from the last blow before you're staggering from the newest one. Will you survive the next week, the next month with this kid? Or are you both going to drown?

Once upon a time, you had idealistic dreams of what the future held. You were going to raise a notable doctor, a teacher, an artist, an engineer. Now those fantasies are long forgotten. You'll be lucky, you think, to produce even a high-school graduate.

The storms of child-raising can rob us of perspective. We forget that we were heading somewhere important. Now we're just clinging to the halyards, gasping for our next breath.

The Megapurpose

If we could step back, calm our fears, and think for sixty seconds about the overall purpose of parenting, we would say (in various wordings) that we are trying to usher this child, this teenager toward a stable adulthood. We want them to grow up to be mature, to make good decisions, to carry their own weight in life, to be responsible. I like to use the term *self-regulating*. By that I mean the state of being independently able to adjust whatever needs adjusting.

People commonly speak about "rules and regulations." In fact, the two are not quite the same. *Rules* are outside dictums meant to control our activity. To *regulate* something, on the other hand, means to adjust it in small increments like a thermostat on your furnace. If the house is getting a little cold, the thermostat senses the chill and turns on the heating mechanism—but only for a little while, until the temperature comes up to a comfortable range. Then the thermostat shuts it off again so as not to overheat the house. It is constantly assessing what's needed and then taking steps to improve it.

Self-regulating adults do the same in all areas of life. They say to themselves, "Hmmm, seems like my pants are getting a little tight.

I'm going to have to regulate my food intake and crank up my exercise routine, aren't I?" Or they say, "This checking account is getting down pretty low, isn't it? Maybe I don't need that big new flat-screen TV quite yet."

Kids who are spinning out of control stand in desperate need, over the long haul, of self-regulation. That's where we are headed with them. We definitely won't get there overnight. They will flip out time and again along the way. But our megapurpose is to move them ever so gradually in the direction of being able to manage themselves appropriately.

This does not mean that every child will grow up to be the same. God has created each one of us to be unique. Some of us are gifted in one area, while others excel in another. We all, regardless of our specialties, need to be self-regulating.

There is, in fact, a common myth in educational and psychological circles called "the well-rounded child." It seeks to make every child good in history and sports and music and science and drama and. . . . This just does not square with reality. If you love a child enough to nurture that child, you will ask the nurturance question, which is "How is this child meant to grow? And what can I do to accelerate that growth?"

Parents who read the Bible frequently quote Proverbs 22:6, which says, "Train up a child in the way he should go: and when he is old, he will not depart from it" (KJV). Actually, the original Hebrew text carries a little more nuance that shows up in The Amplified Bible: "Train up a child in the way he should go and *in keeping with his individual gift or bent. . . .*" (italics added). The Creator has built into each person certain distinct specialties that need to be maximized by those who care for them.

If I happen to love my collection of climbing vines and then somebody gives me a rubber tree plant, it is simply not going to climb up the wall the way it's "supposed to." I may get frustrated over that. "What's the matter with you?" I'll say to the rubber plant. "Get your act together. You're supposed to latch onto the brickwork here and add to this wall of green along with all the other plants."

It just isn't going to happen.

Kids who are fundamentally artistic in nature may never make great scientists. Kids who are developmentally delayed are probably not going to make the honor roll. Kids who are thorough and diligent, weighing every word, are unlikely to become great on-stage comedians. It is unfair to pretend otherwise.

> "Who we are is God's gift to us. What we become is our gift to God."
> —Eleanor Powell

If you have a child who is born to sing or dance, it does no good to snarl, "Go for a real job, will ya? My dad had to work hard in a factory to make a living, and so have I. I'm not scraping up sixty thousand to put you through college so you can just mess around in the arts building for four years." Instead, ask yourself, *What is this kid cut out to do in life?*

Eleanor Powell, stage star of the 1930s, had it right when she said, "Who we are is God's gift to us. What we become is our gift to God." Or to cite a different kind of genius (a Presbyterian minister who taught a class I once took): "We need to understand our *teleology*. That's a complicated concept from the Greek word *telos*— 'the end'—combined with *–ology*, 'the study of.' It means to focus on the goal, the end for which we were created."

He went on to say, "Jesus clearly knew His teleology, His destiny in the world. It was not to become a famous rabbi. It was not to lead a revolt against the Roman occupation. He came to proclaim the kingdom of God, to get in trouble for that proclamation, to die as a sacrifice for the world's redemption, and to rise again in victory. That was what He was all about."

We who are responsible for children, however confused and irritating they may be, must show them *teleological love*, which means to get inside their soul and make it blossom. The more clearly we grasp what they were created to be, the greater progress we can make in bringing them to a responsible, productive, self-regulating adulthood.

From Goals to Logistics

But this is more than a one-sided process. Eventually the mega-purpose has to be realized in visible, manageable segments. For this to happen, we and the child together have to settle on goals in ordinary life. We cannot dictate these goals from the mountaintop based solely upon our superior parental insight. We have to go through the hard work of goal agreement. That is when both parties say, "Let's make sure we do this."

Sometimes we state goals in language that sounds good but means different things to different people. To give an overly simple illustration: What does "clean the kitchen" actually signify? The child imagines one thing while the parent has something far more extensive in mind. "Hey, I'm done with the kitchen, Mom! It's all good." Mom walks in for an inspection and says, "What are you talking about? The counter hasn't been wiped down. There's still gook in the sink—this place isn't even close. . . ." We have a definite lack of goal agreement. (Even husbands don't quite get the full picture sometimes, correct?)

I hear this all the time in the world of mental health. A group of highly trained professionals sit down around a conference table and say, "Now our goal is to do what's in the best interest of the child." It sounds so lofty and good. But the minute you start pressing for definition of what would actually benefit the child in question, the room erupts in discord. Squabbling and fighting go on for the next thirty minutes.

In setting interim goals that will serve effectively from day to day, week to week, and month to month, I have found it useful for parents and kids to use this planning tool, working from the top down:

- The Goal is a general, overarching statement of where we want to end up. It may not be measurable, but it signifies a definite reality that everyone desires.
    - The Objective gives definition to the Goal. It sets benchmarks that tell whether the Goal has been reached or not.
    - The Strategies give the methods for fulfilling the Objective.
    - The Tactics spell out the individual steps we will take in implementing the Strategies.
- The Logistics simply list what has to happen first, second, and third within each Tactic.

Here is an example from the world of business, just to clarify the five levels:

Let's say you're operating a pizza franchise. You say to yourself, "February is coming, and I want to have a really successful month." That is your Goal.

Well, what does "really successful" mean? Does it mean you'll sell one thousand pizzas? Does it mean you'll bring in two hundred first-time customers? Does it mean you'll turn a certain profit? You have to quantify.

If, after some thinking, you say, "I want to clear a ten-thousand-dollar profit after all expenses are paid," now you have a measurable Objective. You will be able to tell whether you have succeeded or failed.

How will you make this happen? What will be your Strategies? You could determine to sell more pizzas to your existing customers than ever before. Or you could stick with the same number of sales, but cut back on the toppings—the number of pepperoni slices per pizza, for example. That would lower your cost of product and thereby increase your financial margin. Or you could advertise like crazy in order to bring in new customers. You could tell all your employees to push hard for add-on sales, like Coke liters and bread-sticks. You could open up a catering branch.

Eventually, you'll have to decide which Strategies are going to get your prime attention.

If you choose to do an advertising blitz, then what will be your Tactics? Hire an ad agency? Get kids to stand out on the curb holding big signs? Put flyers in the local convenience stores by the cash register? Put flyers in every motel room within five miles? These are your possible Tactics.

Finally, you'll have to boil all this down into a to-do list of Logistics: *8:00 a.m. tomorrow—call my partner and tell him how much money I'm planning to spend on this. 9:00 a.m.—contact the advertising agency.* Etc.

The great thing about filling out the pyramid is that it becomes an instant diagnostic tool when things go badly. If at the end of February, you've netted only two thousand dollars instead of ten thousand dollars, you can readily go back and figure out why. Was there a problem with the Objective? Were some of the Strategies flawed? Did you not follow through on some critical Tactics? Where was the blowout that caused the tire to go flat?

One definite difficulty will show up if the plan was built solely by the boss, without input from the employees. If your idea of "a great February" is to clear a ten-thousand-dollar profit while their idea of "a great February" is having everyone's boyfriend or girlfriend stop by each Saturday night for a party on the house, plus three days off to go skiing, you don't have *goal agreement*. It is vitally important to frame the plan together, from top to bottom, in order to achieve the Goal.

School Talk

How does this work in a family with a difficult kid? What is the application to our theme?

Let's illustrate with one of the main hassles faced by parents and guardians: school performance. Nearly every troubled young person is doing badly in the classroom. The conversation in mid-August could start out like this:

"Hey, school starts up in another couple of weeks. Are you looking forward to that?"

"Hardly! Last year was awful. I hate school."

"Would you like it to go better this year, if it could?"

"Yeah. But that's impossible."

(Ignoring the negativity) "What if we set out a goal called 'to have a good year in school'? How does that sound?" (The truth is, no kid *enjoys* failing at school. Nobody likes getting *F*s or staying late for detention. It would be a lot less pain to stay out of trouble, if only there were a plan to do so.)

From this point, the adult pulls out the pyramid chart. The top triangle gets filled in. *GOAL: To have a good year at school.*

"Now what does that look like? In terms of grades—what do you think?"

The kid may respond, "Well, I got Cs last year in P.E. and art. But one or two Fs are OK. Everybody gets at least one, you know. I'm terrible at math."

"But it's important," you may respond.

"No, it's not. I'm never going to use this algebra stuff anyway. Think about it—when you try to help me with math, you have to go back and read the chapter yourself."

Clearly, we don't have agreement at the Objective level.

Our natural instinct is to push back immediately. "No way are you settling for Fs! That's ridiculous. Hey, when I was your age, . . ."

This will only unleash a rebuttal of excuses. "Well, see, my math teacher doesn't like me. . . . I turned in a whole bunch of homework last year, and she lost my papers. It wasn't *my* fault! . . . I was sick one day when there was a test, and she was supposed to give me three days to make it up, but she didn't. . . . The thing is, I was hanging out with So-and-so, and even though we weren't doing anything bad, they hit me with an unexcused absence. . . ." This litany can go on forever, derailing the discussion.

Far better for the adult to say, "You know, you're right—I don't use much calculus in my life these days. I didn't become a scientist, and you may not either. Even so, we're kind of stuck with this math thing to get through school, aren't we? Not much either you or I can do to avoid it. So why don't we come up with a way to handle this? I'll help you. Let's figure out a fresh approach. Would you like a math tutor, for example?"

The two parties are now on the same side of the table, working together to solve a joint challenge. It's like swimming in the ocean. If you get caught in a riptide, the advice of lifeguards is that you *not* try to swim against it. You will only wear yourself out and eventually get sucked underneath. Instead, you swim along *with* the tide, edging slightly sideways whenever you can, until in time you free yourself.

It's the same thing with kids. Don't push into a power struggle if you can help it. Edge in a different direction that the kid can halfway agree with. Work with the resistance, not against it.

Soon the two of you will be aligned on an Objective that will constitute a "good year." It may be as modest as "all Cs and one *D*." As a parent, you would like to have seen something a little more ambitious than that, but take what you can agree upon. Who knows, your young person may get inspired to outperform the standard!

You move immediately into the Strategies. Would tutoring help, for example? Rewards may play a role. This could be a point system that leads to promised payoffs (larger allowance, trip to the ice cream store, a shopping expedition). Or you could hold out the carrot of surprises that will drop out of the sky at unpredictable moments. Another strategy could be interactive learning— the child and you working together instead of slogging it out alone.

Next come the Tactics. "How about doing the math homework first each day to get it out of the way? Everything else will be easier after that, don't you think?" Or, "Here's a bunch of lime-green stickies for you to put on every problem that stumps you. If you can't get the answer, don't sit there and stew about it. Just save it for me when I get home from work. I promise we'll go over your stickies right after supper." You might even offer to set up a special desk or table in the family room for this effort instead of the kid having books sprawled across the bed.

Finally we get down to the level of Logistics. How is the kid going to remember to gather all the right books and papers before leaving school for the day? Does she need a bigger backpack? If her school maintains a Web site with homework specifics, does your child know how to access it when confused about the due date for something? Or shall we build a list of teacher phone numbers for use at such moments? This block of the pyramid, at the bottom, is largest because it has to contain the most details.

Hopefully, grade cards will start to show the fruit of this goal agreement. Your child or teenager will start to experience tiny flickers of success. If not, then the two of you pull out your chart again and say, "Where are we wandering off our plan? Have we used all the Strategies we said we were going to use? Do we need some more Tactics? Are we just getting sloppy on the Logistics?"

Throughout it all, parent and child are swimming together. They both would really like to feel the joy of having a good year at school. United in a common cause, they can make it happen. They're a team; they are no longer at war.

Showdown Averted

This mechanism can be used successfully for a wide range of issues. I have helped parents develop goal agreements with their kids around such things as curfews, drugs, weight control, and sex. They didn't try to "lay down the law" with their headstrong teenager because they knew that would lead only to further rebellion. They instead got on the same side of the table with the kid to empower him toward the right path.

Even something as mundane (but still frustrating!) as keeping a clean bedroom can be processed in this way. Every parent knows the exasperation of walking into a disaster zone. "For crying out loud, I provide this wonderful house for my children, and look at this mess! I wash their clothes, fold them, bring them to the room—and what happens? He doesn't even have the common decency to put them in the drawers. So the clothes sit there on the edge of the bed, get knocked off onto the floor, they get stepped on, and I end up washing the stuff all over again. Aaaaagh!"

A great deal of progress can be gained simply by sitting down together and defining the Objective. What constitutes "a clean bedroom"? Contrary to what young people fear, it does not mean they have to be ready at all times for a *House Beautiful* photographer. It may turn out to be as basic as saying that by the time the kid leaves for school in the morning . . .

- Closet doors are able to be shut. (Whatever chaos rages *behind* the closet door is left to the kid, just so the door is closeable.)
- The floor is free of clothes, shoes, and reading material. In other words, it is now possible to run the vacuum without hindrance.
- The bed is made.

This is not saying that such order has to reign twenty-four hours a day. The kid is free to mess it up, scattering stuff all around, in the afternoon or evening—just so it returns to "clean" status by eight o'clock the next morning.

Logistically, this plan may require some new shelving or a hamper. Fine. Off to Home Depot or Wal-Mart we go. Parent and child work together to achieve a result that both can live with in peace.

The process of setting out a clear goal together and then thinking through the steps to reach it can reap amazing rewards, both short-term and long-term. As we *empower* kids to succeed at challenges large and small, they become whom they want to become deep inside. And they gradually learn the skill of self-regulation.

A Case Study

I have seen this work even in times of intense conflict when everyone was too worked up to sit down with any piece of paper and fill out a pyramid. The steps were enacted regardless—on the fly, so to speak.

I'll never forget Lora, one of our foster parents, who was being driven crazy by the in-your-face resistance of three sisters we had placed in her home. The girls ranged from age fourteen up to eighteen. They clearly didn't like their circumstances and had set a goal to get out of this foster home.

So they would deliberately scratch Lora's furniture. They would mouth off to her. If she said they needed to be home by 9:00 p.m., they'd show up at midnight. They were bucking the system every way they could think of. They wanted to get kicked out.

Lora said to me one day, "This is awful. I can't go on with this. Maybe you'd better put these girls somewhere else."

"Before we do that, bring them into the office, and let's have a talk together," I replied. "Pick them up after school tomorrow, and we'll see what we can do."

> You often can't control the child,
> but you can control the playing field.

The next afternoon, she was waiting by the curb in front of the high school.

"What are you doing here?" the oldest girl hollered through the open window.

"Hop in," Lora said. "We're going to Hope & Home for a meeting."

"No way," the trio responded almost in unison. "Ain't gonna happen."

Lora rolled up the window and called me on her cell phone. "Ross, they won't even get in the car!" she reported.

"OK," I answered. "Has the bus left yet?"

She looked in her rearview mirror and then answered, "Yes."

"Well, they're going to do what they're going to do. But here is what I want *you* to do. Tell the oldest one that, actually, you don't care whether they come with you or not. It's their choice. They can hang out at school the rest of the day if they want, or they can get in the car with you. You're leaving in three minutes. Whether they come with you or not, you drive off and head for the office here. When you arrive without them, I will call the police and report them as runaways. The police will pick them up and take them to Spring Creek (our local juvenile detention center). It's as simple as that.

"Lay out these two options, and then say it again: 'It's up to you, girls. Do whatever you want. I'm leaving now.'"

As I mentioned in an earlier chapter, you often can't control the child, but you can control the playing field. You can set the conditions and then let the players go wherever they perceive to be in their own self-interest. The formula looks like this:

1. Decide on a condition or limitation that you're sure is fair.
2. Communicate it clearly.
3. Then back away. Let what you've said stand on its own without a lot of extra badgering.

Within a few seconds my phone rang again. "Ross, this is Lora. Just thought you'd want to know, we're headed your way. All four of us."

Obviously, nobody was smiling when they entered my office. The girls dropped into their chairs and glared at me. They were furious in their silence.

I started out with a casual tone. "So, hey, I understand that you guys are basically making Lora's life miserable these days. From what I hear, you're doing everything you can to torture my poor foster parent."

"So what do you care about it?" one of them snapped back.

"Tell me what you have in mind," I asked.

"To get out of that hole," the oldest one said, nodding in Lora's direction. "We hate it there." At least they were making their goal clear.

"OK, I hear you. But here's the problem," I said. "I'm the boss of this agency, the one who decides who goes where. And the trouble is, I have nowhere else to put you for at least a week. I might have a different home for you next week—I don't know for sure." In this way I showed a small bit of flexibility, that they weren't chained to Lora forever.

"But before I put you somewhere else, you've got to show me that you can treat a foster parent well. If you can't do that, then there's no reason for me to do you a favor.

"So it's up to you. If you want to walk out the front door right now, go for it. I'll call the cops, they'll pick you up, and Spring Creek will take three or four days to sort you through their system, as you know. Otherwise, you can take my deal, which is to show me that you can handle a foster home without ruining it. The thing is, you're in charge here. You get to decide. I'm just outlining the consequences of your options.

"If you go home again with Lora but keep being jerks to her . . . well, she is a real person, you know? She has real feelings. What do you think it's like for her to see her house getting trashed?" Here I was pulling on their sense of empathy, since they were teenagers. They could understand the foster mom's emotions. "I don't want to see Lora going through all the stuff she's enduring, so I could arrange a change. But it will take me a week, as I said. Or we could just call a halt to this whole foster care thing right now. You make the decision."

The room got quiet. Everybody's mind was working hard.

"Tell me something," I then said, changing the subject. "Is there any moment when you guys actually kind of like hanging out with Lora?"

Another pause. Finally, one of them said, "Yeah, late at night. I come downstairs and talk to her, and it's kind of nice."

"OK, that's good. Anything else?"

The girls came up with one or two other situations that weren't so bad after all.

"Now if you want these good times to continue," I explained, "it will take some strategies that Lora will accept. Let's see if we can come up with them." I pulled out a piece of paper.

We ended up drafting half a dozen rules for coexistence. At one point I appealed to the eighteen-year-old's seniority. "What if we said that if you get your two younger sisters settled down in their rooms for the night by nine-thirty, then Lora will make time for just the two of you to sit and talk? Maybe you could even watch a movie together." She said that would be a fair exchange.

"This is just a matter of giving and taking," I concluded. "If it works, then at the end of the week, I'll see about moving you guys."

> Setting a clear goal together and then thinking through the steps to achieve it can reap amazing rewards.

Lo and behold, by the next Saturday, the hastily arranged goal agreement was bearing fruit. The girls decided they'd rather stay with the devil they knew versus a new devil they didn't know. They remained at Lora's house for another month under far more pleasant circumstances. They learned to cooperate with those who were trying to help them rather than the opposite. In the end, they were able to return to their family of origin and function appropriately.

When adults and kids settle on a *goal* that is to their mutual benefit and figure out specific *methods* of attaining that goal, the deadlock of the past is broken. Success and self-regulation are a little closer. The teleology of the future is giving wise guidance to the present. Showdown is giving way to progress. You might just survive this thunderstorm and reach the restaurant after all.

6

Getting from Here to There

Will Rogers, the famous cowboy philosopher and humorist, attended a military briefing during World War I where a Navy admiral described the perils of the German submarines, or U-boats. Following the lengthy recitation of statistics and assault systems that were ravaging Allied shipping, he opened the floor for questions.

"Tell me," Will Rogers asked in his folksy Oklahoma drawl, "can those subs operate in boiling water?"

"No, I suppose not," came the reply.

"Well, then, you've got your solution," said Rogers. "All you have to do is boil the ocean."

The admiral gave him a blank look. "And how are we supposed to do that?"

"Look," said Will Rogers, "I gave you the idea; now you work out the details."

The plan and execution of goal agreements that we covered in the last chapter may evoke a similar question from harried parents: *Yes, but how am I supposed to make it actually happen? What if my teenager and I fill out the whole chart—but then he won't follow through?*

> If we do not set limits in the early years, the child will never know what structure is.

Eliciting cooperation on a day-to-day basis is the challenge. The "what" begs for the "how." The greatest, most brilliantly worded theories have to be put into reality. When the kid isn't doing what he or she agreed to do—then what?

Three Modes

There is no single answer to this dilemma; instead, it is more helpful to think of three general styles or *modes* that parents can use. They are:

- *Command.* "Do it this way, and do it now." Why? "Because I said so." After all, it's your house and your rules.
- *Collaboration.* "Let's work on this together. What do you think we need to make this happen?"
- *Consignment.* "You know the task we agreed upon. Go for it! I'm sure you can figure out how to pull it off."

The first is a case of "I decide, you obey." The second is "We decide, we follow through." The third is "We set the goal, and you take it from there. Let me know if you hit any snags."

Right away the reader will sense that these three modes correlate with increasing age. On a chart, it looks like this:

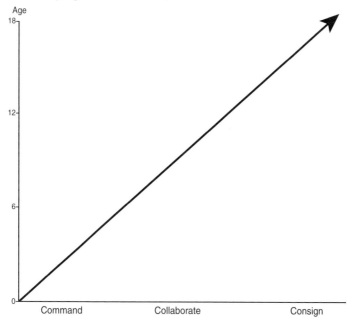

In the early years, the command mode is highly effective as well as necessary. A mom says to her three-year-old, "Pick up your toys, and then you can have your snack." There's no background discussion of *why* the toys should be picked up. The child is simply ordered to do what Mom says, period.

Parents of young children should not feel guilty about being "control freaks." Toddlers need a lot of control! On the other hand, you would not exactly walk into a seventeen-year-old's room and say, "Be ready to leave for church in twenty minutes. Here, I'm laying out the clothes you should wear. Put them on now."

Collaboration comes into usefulness in the middle years of child-hood. A mother asks her seven-year-old to set the table for dinner. The daughter says, "Can I finish watching this cartoon first?" The mother answers, "Yes, that's all right. There will still be time before we sit down to eat." In this case, both parties have given their thoughts, and a win-win solution emerged.

With increasing maturity the use of consignment is appropriate. It's just like going to a consignment store. You turn over your clothing or household appliance to the manager, and you come back a week later to see if it's sold or not. The store personnel, in the meantime, have taken charge of displaying it, answering customer questions, collecting any proceeds, and keeping accurate records for your inspection. The goods were still yours throughout the week, but they were being controlled by your designees.

The strategy for parents is to move their choice of mode *from left to right* as the years increase. This is part of preparing the young person for independence. It is empowering the son or daughter to handle life on their own.

Oddly enough, some parents fall into the trap of the exact opposite! They try to push the arrow from right to left. When their kids are little, they don't feel like cracking down; after all, the little cherubs are just so cute. "Wouldn't you like to take your nap? Oh, well, that's OK; I don't want to make you cry." Life rolls on in an overly permissive vein—until puberty arrives. The kid turns twelve or thirteen, and suddenly the parent gets scared. The stakes are much higher now. *Oh my goodness—I've got to put some firm controls on this kid! If I don't, she's going to get pregnant or get arrested or . . .* And the teenager is left saying, "What's up with the rules all of a sudden? My dad is freaking out."

If we do not set limits in the early years, the child will never know what structure is. And when he reaches the high-risk period of life, he won't know how to self-impose structure. The time for firm, wise commands is at the beginning with gradual loosening of the ropes as the years go by.

Command mode is like being a *sergeant*. You may not bark as loudly, but you leave no doubt about the fact that you're in charge, you meant what you said, and that's that.

Collaboration mode is like being a *coach*. You stick right alongside the player, complimenting what he's doing well and showing what he could do better. You make sure he doesn't get hurt in the process, but you push him to excel.

Consignment mode is like being a college *professor*. You set the course outline, you make yourself available for consultation during office hours, and then you let the students study whenever and wherever they choose. The ball is pretty much in their court. They do know, however, that you'll be giving them a grade at semester's end.

Which Is Your Favorite Mode?

Probably every parent, by instinct, prefers one mode over the other two. Some of us are just naturally command people. We're built to take charge and make the train run on time. We know that kids need firm guidance, and we have no qualms about giving it to them.

This kind of parent does well with preschoolers. Nurses who have kids of their own are great at this. They're organized, they know what needs to happen when, and they say so clearly. Military personnel (whether male or female) are another example because they live in a command-and-control world. They automatically bring it home with them.

When parenting gets a little more complex in subsequent years, however, the command personality may struggle.

Other parents love to coach. They're fascinated with their child's potential for growth, and they delight in bringing it out. The name of the game for them is development. Training is their forte.

Still other parents (perhaps in reaction to their own high-control upbringing) lean in the direction of hands-off. Just tell the kid what you expect, and then back away. They like the consignment mode.

Whatever your personal preferences, I have a bit of blunt news for you: *You need to become good at all three modes.* They're all critical at various times. You can't use one style all the way through. Whichever two modes are weaker for you still need your attention so you can connect with kids in a healthy way.

Backtracking

In fact, it's often necessary to switch back and forth along the continuum. The arrow never quite goes in a straight line for eighteen years. When kids regress or fall down, parents have to accommodate their current mind-set.

Suppose your family is getting ready to go on vacation. "I'm going to take off work early on Friday so we can head out and beat the traffic," you announce. "Everybody have your stuff packed by noon."

If Mom stops by the sixteen-year-old's room at ten-thirty and says, "How's it going?" she will most likely get a curt "Don't baby me! I know what 'noon' means. I'll be ready."

But what if noon arrives and a bunch of the teenager's clothes are still in the washer, not yet dried? What if the swimsuit is still over at a friend's house where it was left after last week's pool party? And oh, by the way, the kid needs to make a quick run to Walgreens for a couple of supplies. . . .

You'll be frustrated, no doubt. You won't be pulling out of the driveway until one o'clock or later. It is entirely appropriate to say to your teen, "You know what? Next time we'll collaborate on this kind of thing. Two days ahead of time, we'll sit down together and make a list of all the stuff you want to take on vacation. We'll analyze what's readily on hand and what isn't. We'll get a jump on this process."

There is no shame in collaboration. You can assure your teenager that if this goes well, the subsequent trip will return to on-your-own packing. A temporary adjustment is needed—that's all.

Meanwhile, your ten-year-old may need *more* than collaboration. If the list isn't getting checked off, you may need to stand over his shoulder at eleven o'clock and start giving commands: "OK, put this in here. Put that over there. Pick this up. Go make this one last phone call."

But on the other hand, if the ten-year-old does well with collaboration, you may want to say, "Good job! In fact, next time I think you can handle this packing thing without having me help you make the list. You're really managing your life better all the time."

To cite a different example: if the goal agreement pyramid called for a clean bedroom (clearly defined) each morning before school, but it hasn't happened for three days in a row, the child is showing that he or she can't handle consignment. It's time to backtrack. You come in that evening, sit on the bed, and say, "You know what? This room thing isn't working, is it? Do you need to set your alarm a little earlier so you have time?"

You may get a dodge statement in reply. "Well, see, I'd just hit the snooze button anyway because I'd know I didn't *really* have to get up yet. That wouldn't help."

"OK, then I tell you what: I'll start coming back at seven-forty every morning before you have to leave, and we'll pick up your room together. We'll collaborate on this."

Most kids—especially girls—will be horrified by the idea of Dad helping to collect their whatevers lying around. A few boys may kind of like the extra attention, but not for long. Ultimately, it will drive them crazy. They'll be pleading for consignment again.

If not, you may have to move all the way back to command mode. "Son, I'll be showing up every morning at six-thirty to roll your body out of bed onto the floor. We'll go through your laundry together, and I'll tell you where to put it. If the process drags out so long that you miss the school bus, you'll be walking, pal."

Every parent has to become proficient in using all three modes. You can't stick to your favorite and ignore the other two or expect your spouse to cover for you. Your child needs the nuanced guidance of all three.

Some command-mode parents fear that as they move up the continuum, they'll be losing control. Not so. When you put your clothes at a consignment store, have you lost control? No. You've simply delegated control to others according to your parameters. The same is true in parenting.

> You can't stick to your favorite mode
> and ignore the other two.
> Your child needs all three.

Command mode, admittedly, is the most time-efficient. You don't have to fiddle around with long-winded negotiation; you just declare how things are going to be, and that's that. But command mode has other downsides. It can trigger increasing resistance as the years go by and the child wants to participate in the decision.

The other two modes (collaboration especially) take longer on the front end. The dialogue flows back and forth. But the time invested is worth it in moving the child toward self-regulation.

At the beginning of life, parents hold all the cards in the game. They can totally dominate the field of play. As the child grows and matures, we begin to give them cards, one at a time. The child can then play the cards as they see fit. If they mess up, it is entirely appropriate for us to take a card back. But over time, our goal is to reach the point when the son or daughter, now on the edge of adulthood, is holding all the cards. They are ready to use them wisely—and even to start handing them along to *their* children in the future.

Choosing the Right Mode

In deciding which mode to employ—and especially whether a backtrack is needed—three strategic questions help to clarify the situation. By silently running these through your head, you can make a decision on which tool to use when you open your mouth.

1. How important is this?

Does it really matter whether the parent's way prevails or not? Or are we just jerking people around for our own comfort? Hair length or color, for example, is perhaps not the end of the world that some parents think it is. I heard about one couple whose teenager wanted to dye her hair a bright magenta shade. Naturally, they would have preferred that she not do that. But they wisely said to her, "It's up to you. The only thing we would require is that if you do this, people *are* going to make remarks about it—and you have to field those remarks calmly and maturely. You can't be getting into arguments and spitting matches with them. You have to be prepared for whatever flak comes your way and not lose your cool."

The matter of wearing seat belts, on the other hand, *is* important. Parents can't afford to be laissez-faire about that. Which brings us to the second question.

2. Do I need the kid's buy-in?

In order to reach the desired result, is it necessary to secure the child's willing cooperation? Or can you pull this off unilaterally?

With a five-year-old you can give a straight command: "Buckle up, Michael. The car is not going to move an inch until you do." If Michael still won't comply, you get out of your seat, go around to his, and snap the belt into place yourself, announcing a stern consequence if he messes with it.

But when he grows up to age sixteen and gets his driver's license, the time for collaboration has come. You still want him to wear his seat belt (now more than ever!), while he may be fairly nonchalant about it. You sit down together and say, "I'm really excited that you're going to get to drive now! This is a great day. You'll be using my car, of course. And it's important to me that you wear your seat belt 100 percent of the time. Do you think you can go along with me on that?" Most teens, eager for the keys, will say yes.

When Michael goes off to college, however, this collaborative agreement may fade into the background. What if his younger brother comes back from a campus visit and reports that seat belts are now being ignored? You need Michael's buy-in on this issue. The conversation could go this direction: "You know where I stand on wearing seat belts, of course. We don't have to go over that again. And now, you're at the point in life where this is pretty much your decision. I have no choice but to let you make the call. I do need to say, however, that if you choose not to wear your seat belt, I'm not going to keep paying my portion of your car insurance. The risk to our family rates is too great if something bad happens—not to mention the risk to your life. I need to back away from the insurance arrangement. Again, you decide." You have consigned the matter to him for handling. You have recognized that you can't control a situation if the levers of control are beyond your reach.

Leaders in all arenas of life have to take note of whether buy-in is necessary or not. How many times at work has the boss said, "Let's have a meeting and discuss such-and-such a policy" when in fact his mind was already made up. If the senior executives have already decided that employees are going to have to pick up another 15 percent of the group health insurance premiums, then what's the point of debating it in a lengthy meeting? On the other hand, a proposal to work four hours of overtime each Saturday morning for the next three months due to an output crunch definitely requires the willingness of the employees. If they won't come in, the plan falls to the ground. Buy-in is crucial.

The government does all kinds of advertising to get our buy-in on certain things. Television commercials urge us to stop smoking, to donate money for worthy causes, to volunteer our time. But have you ever seen a commercial from the IRS saying, "Please file your taxes"? Hardly. Everybody knows this is mandatory, and harsh penalties apply to those who don't.

If something is important and nonnegotiable, the parent handles it in a different way from that which is debatable and optional.

3. *How much time do I have?*

As mentioned before, collaboration and consignment take more time to set up than straight commands. Sometimes there simply isn't enough time for a dialogue. You need to get the issue settled *now*. If your ten-year-old and his buddy have gotten the bright idea to hoist their bicycles up onto the roof and are riding them there, you have to take action immediately. "Stop! Get down here right now!"

Sometimes, however, adults say they're too busy to talk with their kids when it's rather a matter of priorities. We need to put the briefcase away, turn the TV off, and engage their young minds. If we never have time, we're never going to cultivate this child toward maturity. They'll never learn how to process decisions on their own. The skill of weighing pros and cons and coming to an intelligent conclusion will always be stunted.

A Job to Fulfill

Parenting is a big job, isn't it? Figuring out how to mix the proper amounts of command, collaboration, and consignment over the years is a dynamic and complex task. We never quite get the luxury of going onto autopilot.

More than once I've sat listening to agitated parents telling me a litany of awful things their child is doing. "You won't believe what happened the other day . . .," they say, launching into gory details. Eventually I stop them to ask: "Now, how old is this boy?"

"He just turned fourteen."

"Hmmm," I say. "Sounds to me like you've got a fourteen-year-old boy on your hands!" In other words, he's acting about normal—or at least average—for that stage of growing up.

"Now, what's *your* job? You are the adults in this scenario. You're the ones with the experience, the history, the maturity—and the responsibility. It's your show to manage."

Like it or not, children look to us for answers. They expect us to know what to do. Even though they hotly disagree with us at times, they still turn our way for protection, for guidance, for encouragement, and most of all, for nurturance. As we mold their pliable hearts and minds, we fulfill our highest calling. And the world reaps the benefit for generations to come.

CHAPTER

7

"Bad to the Bone?" Not Entirely

Every parent or guardian of a seriously off-track young person rides a roller coaster of emotions. Sometimes you're encouraged; you can see real progress. But soon thereafter (usually about three o'clock in the morning), you can descend into a pit of despair. Nothing is going right. Your kid is bucking you on every possible front. He won't study. He chooses all the wrong friends. His language is getting worse, not better. His music is driving you crazy. He won't pick up his room. He's got this new tattoo. He's determined to make life conform to his terms—which is a sure road to disaster.

In the words of the signature song from George Thorogood and the Destroyers, this kid is "bad to the bone."

I know the feeling well. I've seen fifth-graders who knew more about sex, drugs, and violence than I did as a fairly well-educated adult. One eight-year-old in our program threatened the foster parents with talk of hammers and knives so convincingly that the couple felt they needed to lock their bedroom door at night. Even a three-year-old had to be removed from one foster home because he was too dangerous to the infant who lived there.

Whenever I'm tempted to write off a kid as completely incorrigible, however, I take a deep breath and remember something I learned from a Yellowstone National Park tour guide. My older daughter, Alexann, and I were on a motorcycle trip together—something I did for both girls when they turned ten years old. We had a great time on the road together, and one afternoon we were riding horses near Yellowstone Lake. Our guide was a Native American, which made it all the more interesting; I'm Cherokee myself, and my wife is Anishanabe (more commonly known as Chippewa).

At one point, he raised his hand and said, "Hold up. See that bison on the path? We need to wait until he moves along." I squinted toward the horizon and could barely make out the shaggy shape at least a quarter mile away.

I sat there on my horse in the hot sun, waiting. Something didn't make sense. "I guess I'm a little confused," I said to the guide. "Last night we stayed in one of the big camps here in the park, and there were bison all over the place, it seemed. You could walk right up close to them."

The guide shook his head. "Yes, I know—it's crazy," he answered. "I'm just telling you, these are big animals that need their space. None of *my* tour groups is going to crowd them, that's for sure."

Soon he was telling a story. Not long before, a bear had wandered into one of the camps, and the tourists had gathered around to gawk and take pictures. One woman brought out a bag of marshmallows. She tossed them one at a time into the air, and the bear caught them in its mouth. Shutters snapped and camcorders rolled to catch the action. What a wonderful, delightful bear, everyone said.

The bear stood up on its hind legs and pawed the air, clowning as if in a circus. The marshmallows kept coming, and the bear kept dancing to get them. The crowd applauded. "Isn't this just the greatest bear?" they said to one another. "He's funny; he's hysterical."

And then . . . the woman ran out of marshmallows. "Sorry, they're all gone," she said. The bear came back down onto all fours and moved closer to her. He did not seem to be happy about the absence of treats. The crowd grew quieter. All of a sudden, the bear raised one forepaw and, with a mighty thrust, backhanded the woman to the ground, breaking her neck. He then went rambling off into the trees.

People screamed. "Help!" they yelled. The woman writhed in excruciating pain. "Go get a ranger!" somebody said. "Gotta shoot that bear before somebody else gets hurt!" The crowd was united in its opinion: What a horrible, mean, dangerous bear to be up so close to a campsite.

Turning back to my daughter and me, the Indian guide said simply, "You know what? Same bear."

He was absolutely right. The bear had not changed at all. Only the incentive system had changed. People were trying to claim that the bear had undergone a massive personality switch in ten seconds when in fact the only change was in the tourists' behavior.

This was an epiphany moment for me as I reflected on my job as a supervisor. At that time, I was in charge of a department of some 250 employees. All too often I'd listened to managers say, "Hey, Ross, take a look at this resumé. This person is fantastic. I really want to hire him. In fact, can you help me out on the salary? We need to bump up the pay scale a bit in this case, so I can get this incredible person, OK?"

And then, just six months later, the story had swung around 180 degrees. "This person is just awful. He does this and this and this and this. We've got to fire him. Please sign this dismissal form, Ross."

I would scratch my head and say, "Hmmm, is this the same person who looked so terrific not long ago?"

Yes, it was the "same bear." Something about our performance environment had not taken advantage of his strengths or perhaps even turned his strengths into weaknesses.

Finding the Best Route

Many a parent gets swept up in this kind of whiplash. The kid who says, "I love you" is suddenly screaming, "I hate you!" It makes no sense. Can she truly love you even though she's currently throwing a fit about something?

The answer is yes. This teenager has not developed some kind of split personality. The pressures of adolescent life have drawn out a stormy reaction. Meanwhile, the challenge for adults is to calm down, stop jumping to conclusions, and ask ourselves, "Just what is this bear really? What in the environment is setting her off? What are the strengths I can maximize?"

The most obnoxious kid in the world has the capacity to be an achiever for good—at something. The truth is, everybody would like to succeed. Nobody wants to be a failure. If some adult could help this young person find an avenue for achievement, he would be glad to travel that road. It's always more fun in life to get compliments than criticisms.

But the avenue has to match up well with the kid's abilities and interests. Put it this way: If you're looking for an animal that can really fly high in the sky, you wouldn't choose a bear. If the child in your home is inclined toward weight gain, the road of gymnastics is probably not the best choice. We who guide them need to analyze their natural inclinations and figure out what avenues of achievement are most conducive. If the first idea doesn't work out, then maybe the second one will. Or the third.

Close your eyes for a minute and review the route from your workplace to your home. You know it well; you drive it every evening at five o'clock. You pull out of the company parking lot, turn left toward the interstate, then take the on-ramp heading east. It's so familiar you don't even consciously think about it anymore.

But what if something blocks your way on a given evening? What if there's a bad accident on the highway? Or what if road construction has begun? Can you get home a different way?

Of course. You sort through the various alternate routes in your mind and choose the best one.

The same skill is needed in parenting. If the normal avenue isn't working for your teenager, start scouting alternatives. Don't just let the kid sit in traffic getting frustrated. Whatever it takes, get them home safely and in a fairly positive frame of mind.

> The most obnoxious kid in the world
> has the capacity to be an achiever
> for good—at something.

If you want to think of a truly tough traffic challenge, try the halls of any junior high school. The kid we've always loved and cared for is suddenly hit with a blitz of social demands. Voices on every side are insisting that he or she look just right, sound cool, defend himself against all threats, and show the ability to compete.

Developmental psychologists tell us that one of the most important things for any person is to have a sense of mastery (or at least control) over their environment. A child or teenager—or even an adult—needs to be able to say to himself, *I can handle this. I know what to do.* That is why, in the wake of a serious accident, the therapy of video games can actually do a lot of good. The victim may be so injured he can move only a finger—but that's enough to let him steer the on-screen figure through the maze. The player feels not so helpless. He can achieve something after all.

When we help our children build on their strengths, rather than condemning them for their many weaknesses, we set them up to succeed. We enhance their sense of purpose in life. Maybe they're not just a useless wart on the face of the planet after all. Maybe they have a contribution to offer, a goal to pursue, a reason to take up space. After all, their mom or dad thinks they're valuable.

The avenue of achievement does not have to be large. In fact, small achievements can deliver just as much of a life-affirming message as big ones. The wise parent takes any accomplishment— as modest as remembering to make the bed each morning without having to be told—and uses it as an opportunity to invest in the child. "Hey, you're doing really well at taking care of your room. Way to go!" This supercharges the engine of performance for the future.

Reseeding the Forest

But what if there seems to be absolutely nothing to affirm in a child? Frustrated parents have said to me, "My kid doesn't do one positive thing. In fact, he doesn't even like anything. I don't have anything to take away as a form of discipline. I don't have any hooks into his life."

I respond by comparing the child to a burned-over forest. Everything green has been turned to ashes. There's nothing left to grow, it seems. All is empty and barren.

This is not only sad but also dangerous, as we pointed out in chapter 3. People who feel bankrupt, with nothing left to lose, become volatile. They can torment the lives of everyone around them.

"The first thing you've got to do," I tell the worried parents or foster parents, "is to reseed the forest. This comes even before we talk about discipline or setting limits. You've got to put back into this child's life something of value. This will lead to new goals."

I was talking to one set of parents with a daughter I'll call Vanessa, who had absolutely "gone on strike" when it came to obeying her parents. She refused to do anything they asked. They had tried every tactic in the book, they thought. I began emphasizing the reseeding concept. What could we offer that Vanessa would respond to?

We decided to ask her. "What are some activities other kids do that you think might be fun? What's something new that you'd like in your life?" We even gave her a list of things to prime the pump. After some discussion, she settled on gymnastics. She said she'd like to go flying through the air above the parallel bars. (Such a statement contradicted the parents' earlier view that she didn't care about anything in life.)

"Good choice," we all said. "Let's go after this."

The process, of course, would involve gymnastics classes. And Vanessa would get to go shopping for some of those sparkly (and expensive) outfits. The family could subscribe to gymnastics magazines. Soon she would have the chance to compete in local gymnastics meets.

(It helped, in this case, that we were located in Colorado Springs, home to the US Olympic Training Center. Some of the world's best gymnasts were there on display, working on their routines. Vanessa's parents jumped at the chance to take their daughter for the free tour where they could watch from the balcony while the athletes worked out.)

"Don't attach any demands or requirements at the beginning," I instructed Mom and Dad. "Just get her hooked on the joy of gymnastics. Let the green shoots start to come up out of the burned ground for a while. Your stance is entirely in the mode of 'We're going to help you achieve. We're going to work with you to figure out the avenues that get you to success.'

"The day will come, believe me, when she is excited enough about gymnastics that you can start leveraging it. You'll be able to say, 'There's a big meet coming up in Kansas City next month. We really want to take you there. Now in order for you to go on this trip, we need for you to take care of the following three things,' and you spell out some of the performance issues you've been waiting to correct. But the love of gymnastics has to be strong enough to make the desired behaviors worthwhile."

> If you don't know what somebody
> wants, either you're not listening,
> or you're not asking.

Within a year, Vanessa had become a much happier as well as a more cooperative teenager. She had a vested interest in life after all, and her parents were on her side in enabling her to reach her goals.

The fact that she had gotten to select the sport in the beginning was absolutely crucial. Nobody imposed gymnastics upon her from above. She picked out something meaningful to her, and adults opened up the avenues that headed that way.

An old adage says, "If you don't know what somebody wants, either you're not listening, or you're not asking." Everybody harbors quiet fantasies of what they'd like to do. These need to be surfaced for their potential to reseed the forest.

I once heard about a high school shop teacher who was like none other. Too many shop teachers say to their students on the first day of the semester, "OK, now for the next four weeks we're going to learn the tools. This is a jigsaw. This is a band saw. This is a plane. I'll pass out schematic drawings of each one of them, and you will fill in all the part names. . . . Here are the safety drills. Keep your fingers away from all moving parts. Wear your goggles at all times. I don't want anybody getting hurt in this class. . . ." And the students are bored out of their minds. They're miserable.

This shop teacher was the opposite. On the first day of class, he stood up and said, "OK, guys, what do you want to build? Think of anything made out of wood—what should we work on together?"

Wouldn't you know, some wise guy said, "Let's build a piano!" Immediately everybody else jumped in with, "Yeah, a piano! That would be way cool!"

The teacher didn't flinch, and he didn't veto the idea. "Well, that's an enormous project," he said, "but if you want to go for it, we can definitely give it a shot."

The goal was thereby settled. "Now, guess what," the teacher continued, "we're going to need to choose the right wood for this. Here is a piece of pine, which is abundant; it's used for building houses, and it's fairly affordable. But it's too soft for this job. Pine wouldn't stand up to the pressure once we start tightening the strings. So we're going to have to go for one of the hardwoods. . . ." Every student in the class was paying close attention to this lecture on the various kinds of woods because they had a goal in mind.

As the days and weeks went on, every tool in the shop got its explanation, not because it was part of some committee's boring curriculum but because the class needed the function of that tool in order to make the piano. The kids *wanted* to know what a miter saw and a drill and a pair of C-clamps could contribute to their goal. By the end of the semester, this class had actually produced a working musical instrument. They were incredibly proud of it. And more importantly, they had learned how to use all the tools, sequencing the steps of the job and working together as a team.

The same dynamic can happen in a home as well. When kids find out they can be the "carpenter" and select the project—whether it's basketball, watercolor painting, or rabbit-raising—they start down a path that leads to achievement. And their parents are right there beside them, helping make it happen.

I mentioned in an earlier chapter the value of quarterly talent shows at the residential treatment facility I managed. The staff, in the beginning, thought I was crazy. But I said, "No. Remember the proverb about 'idle hands.' Instead of these kids spending their creativity thinking up escape plots—how to get out of this place in the middle of the night—I want them building sets for the talent show and writing scripts and practicing songs. Let's give them a place to show off that's positive. Let's highlight the strengths they have."

So many troubled kids totally shut down because they assume they are locked in a cul-de-sac. Everywhere they turn, they feel blocked. If someone would turn their shoulders around to face the exit—the avenue of achievement—that leads to a different reality, they would gladly take it. Anything to get out of the present trap.

Handling the Misguided

If you give a kid an open choice, there is always the chance, of course, that he will choose something negative. A thirteen-year-old boy who loves video games may say, "Yeah, I want to become the master of Grand Theft Auto." A fifteen-year-old girl may say, "I want to build my own Web site with a live camera feed so I can meet lots of guys."

No responsible adult can agree to these pursuits. But you can quickly counter-offer with something similar that doesn't carry the dark baggage. "You know, I've always wanted to learn some video games myself. Would you teach me? How about if we start with Star Wars? I'm an old geezer, you know, so you have to go slow with me in the beginning." Over the coming weeks, you build a friendship at the computer doing wholesome stuff, and it's so much fun that the two of you don't even remember to get back to Grand Theft Auto.

To the girl you say, "Well, hey, why put pictures of yourself on the Internet when you could do the same thing in real life and even make some money at it? What about some modeling classes to get you started? Let's check out what's available."

Any new venture is both attractive and a little bit scary for kids. They want to jump in and have fun, but they're also afraid of failing. It pays for us to give them time to warm up gradually. I once had a group of kids who said they wanted to form a swim team. One boy, though a decent swimmer, balked at the idea of taking off his clothes in the locker room with the other boys. He was terribly self-conscious about how he looked at that age.

"Fine," I said. "You be the timer on this team. You clock everybody else's performance in the water and keep all the records." He was happy and relieved with that role.

Within one week, however, he was jumping into the pool and swimming like everyone else. In the absence of pressure, he quickly ditched his phobia about undressing. He wanted to get his name on the chart with the others. He had found his avenue for achievement after all.

The human spirit is created with a need to be valued. Every person wants to say on the inside, *Boy, without me this thing wouldn't work, would it? I'm really necessary to the operation. I'm important.*

This does not have to be true of every arena in life. Most of us are willing to admit that we're inept and unskilled in half a dozen different pursuits—so long as we know we can shine in one or two. I openly admit that I can't sing a note, I'm a sloppy painter, and my color blindness means I dare not pick out my own clothes. But let the world know that I *do* know how to resolve conflicts fairly well, and I show love consistently to my family. I can hold my head high because of that.

Kids in distress need the same thing. They need to be proud of *something* in their life. And that pride emerges from their travels on the roads we have put in front of them.

One of the blessings of being raised on a farm is that you get to see the physical results of your efforts. Whether you're raising strawberries or raising a calf, the growth is right there in front of your eyes. You can look at the result and pat yourself on the back. *I made that happen!*

City kids sometimes suffer from the lack of verification for their efforts. Those of us who love them and guide their lives need to keep this in mind, finding ways to demonstrate that they really did cause a difference. Their exertion amounted to something real—and we noticed. This gives a reason for the kid to keep applying effort in the future.

The Illustrated Journal

I will never forget a fifteen-year-old in our psychiatric in-patient unit whom I will refer to as Shannah. She was extremely depressed; she had basically isolated herself and was borderline suicidal.

Both parents had died of AIDS; in fact, I had flown with her to a Chicago hospital so she could say good-bye to her mother in her final days. Shannah was angry with her mother not only for exposing herself to HIV but also because she kept drinking heavily and abusing drugs thereafter, which only accelerated her decline.

In the following months, the girl became sullen. She virtually stopped eating. The staff members were seriously concerned about her, and so was I. What could we do to pull Shannah back from the brink?

She wasn't going to open up and talk to us, that was for sure. Her silence was an iron wall.

Somewhat in desperation, we bought her a journal. "Here's a gift for you, Shannah," we said. "It's a place for you to write down what's going on, what you're thinking about." She accepted it with little comment.

A few days later we said, "Hey, can we see how your writing is going?" We held our breath to see if she would be willing to share it. Thankfully, she pulled out her journal and let us read it. It was actually quite eloquent in describing the pathos of her life.

"Shannah, this is great work!" we exclaimed. "You're doing a phenomenal job. You're actually a good writer—have you thought about doing that for a career?" She smiled weakly but, again, made no response.

This kept going for several weeks. We learned more and more of the turmoil and resentment within her. Then a new brainstorm hit me. "Shannah, what if I got you a camera so you can take some pictures to illustrate your journal?" I asked. "You could think about what would give the visual impression of what you're writing, and then you could add that to the pages."

"I wouldn't know how to use it," she said.

"Well, maybe we could get you into a photography class," I answered. It wasn't long before she was learning all about f-stops and depth of field and shutter speeds. Her photos turned out to be as sensitively composed as her writing.

Going to the class, of course, meant that she had to come out of her shell a bit more. She knew she would be with kids she didn't know in the beginning, and so maybe she ought to take a shower and fix her hair after all. We didn't have to say a word. We didn't need to stand at her door and nag her, "Come on, Shannah—get up! You've got to eat. You've got to put on some decent clothes and do your makeup." No confrontation was necessary. We were on her side. We had aligned with her, empowering her to grow in the area of creative expression.

> The girl who had originally wanted the whole world to leave her alone was now teaching others.

Soon she was writing poetry and joined a poets club. By now she had been able to move out of our institution to a foster home. In time she got involved in showing younger kids how to take photos and create layouts to accompany their writing. The girl who had originally wanted the whole world to leave her alone was now teaching other people how to do things.

She gained weight and became quite talkative. She developed a wry sense of humor, teasing the staff from time to time with great delight. During the last trip to Chicago to take her back to a relative's house for good, I neglected to bring cash while we were driving on the Illinois Tollway; at every toll booth I had to borrow coins from Shannah. For some reason she found that to be hilarious. We had funded her care; now she was funding us!

She continued to do well as adulthood approached. All she needed was an avenue for achievement. She needed someone to invest in her long enough to discern what kind of "bear" she truly was and how she could express her God-given gifts.

The most reclusive, angry, or disruptive young person is, I believe, still within reach of caring adults who will take the time to find out their unique abilities and then open up a road to explore them.

About two-thirds of the way through the French children's classic *The Little Prince*, the lead character finally has a life-altering encounter with the fox. The two cannot play together, the fox insists, because "I am not tamed." He suggests that the little prince might do the job, but the prince doesn't know what "tame" means. The fox explains:

> It is an act too often neglected. . . . It means to establish ties. . . . To me, you are still nothing more than a little boy who is just like a hundred thousand other little boys. And I have no need of you. And you, on your part, have no need of me. To you, I am nothing more than a fox like a hundred thousand other foxes. But if you tame me, then we shall need each other. To me, you will be unique in all the world.[1]

The fox explains a bit later that taming is a lengthy process. It doesn't happen to the impatient.

> First you will sit down at a little distance from me—like that—in the grass. I shall look at you out of the corner of my eye, and you will say nothing. Words are the source of misunderstandings. But you will sit a little closer to me, every day.[2]

I have known hundreds, yes, thousands of children and teen-agers over the years who, though hard on the outside, were inwardly pleading to be tamed. They longed to be pulled out of their isolation. They longed for someone to need them after all, and to show it.

As we sit closer and closer to these young people, gradually earn-ing their trust and studying their uniquenesses, we find out they are not bad to the bone after all. They are children in whom talent lies sleeping and potential lies unnoticed. They are waiting for us to fig-ure out the mystery and guide them to their field of achievement.

8

Inspired to Perform

Everybody's heard of Pavlov's dog—how a Russian physiologist got the animal to salivate solely by producing a sound (footsteps, or a metronome) that had previously been associated with feeding time. Pavlov's formal name for this phenomenon was *classical conditioning*. He won a Nobel Prize in 1904 for his research.

If only we could adjust kids so easily!

Around the same time an American psychologist at Columbia University in New York City was working not with dogs but with cats. Edward L. Thorndike put them in maze boxes and timed how long it took them to find their way out. They would bang into walls and hit dead ends until they eventually stumbled upon the pathways that led to the exit. What Thorndike found interesting was that over a period of days, the cats got smarter. They learned which routes to take and which to avoid, getting out of the maze boxes in less time. He called this *operant conditioning* since the "operator" (the cat) had some influence over the result.

All of us who work with troubled kids wish fervently that they would wise up to the reality of what works in life and what's a dead end. We hate to see them keep banging their heads into hard surfaces. We know they are blessed with a brain far greater than that of a dog or a cat. We want to see them start making better choices.

We know we can't change their behavior unilaterally. (Most of us have certainly tried!) But what we can do is reorganize the playing field so they start to see better, faster ways to win. We can set up the boundaries and markers so that we *reinforce* good moves on their part and *extinguish* bad moves. This is really all there is to conditioning.

Four Options

How many tools do we have for reinforcing and extinguishing? Basically, just four. They are:

1. We can give them something good.
2. We can take away something good.
3. We can give something bad.
4. We can take away something bad.

For parents the examples are easy to see. *Giving something good* means rewarding the child with a compliment, a physical gift of some kind (toys, clothes, money), a privilege, a new freedom—the possibilities are endless.

Taking away something good is saying, "OK, no TV for you" (or allowance, or Internet, or use of the car, or something else the child values) for a certain block of time.

Giving something bad includes a range all the way from additional chores to requiring a written apology to yelling at the kid to spanking him.

Taking away something bad means giving a reprieve from what the child was already dreading. "Guess what—I've decided you don't have to wash windows this Saturday after all."

Most parents I know instinctively track toward the middle two options: *taking away something good* and *giving something bad*. These two seem to get the most immediate results. "Brian, you're grounded for a week." "OK, Ashley, you'll be scrubbing down the barbecue alone tonight while your sister has fun." In these ways, we hope to extinguish undesirable behavior in the future.

What we often don't realize—and research has proven over-whelmingly—is that the most powerful tool of the four is the first one: *Giving something good.* Have we already forgotten the marvelous power of a simple ice cream cone? When you're five years old, that is a very big deal. Children will change all kinds of behavior just to get it. In the following years, as they get older, the definition of *good* evolves, of course. But the dynamic remains the same. Rewarding positive behavior (we'll talk more deeply about this in chapter 9) is a huge motivator.

At the opposite end, the weakest of the four tools is number four: *Taking away something bad.* It is usually too obscure and long-term to make much of a difference. The child may be momentarily relieved, but the impact soon fades.

We have to remember three factors that affect the success of any tactic or action we take as parents: (1) immediacy, (2) relevance, and (3) intensity. An *immediate* response to a problem is always more force-ful than one that is delayed for three days, when the kid has already forgotten what he did wrong. Similarly, a response that *relates* to the infraction carries more force than something disconnected; "the pun-ishment should fit the crime." Finally and obviously, a *strong* move by the parent is better than a weak one that the kid can just brush off.

These three qualities help us gauge whether our use of any of the four tools is going to be effective or not.

Whacked Out

If all of this seems terribly boring and basic so far, you would be surprised how many performance systems of our world are messed up—not just at home but in the workplace, the community, and all around. As Clare Boothe Luce, the famous editor, playwright, satirist, congresswoman, and ambassador, put it wittily, "No good deed goes unpunished."

An employee says to the boss, "Hey, I was just thinking about our system for such-and-such, and I came up with an idea to make it better."

"What's that?" the boss wants to know.

"Well, we could do this, that, and the other."

"Fine. You're in charge of a task force to implement it."

The employee says to himself, *Boy, that's the last time I volunteer one of my good ideas!*

I used to work in hospital systems, and I couldn't help noticing the reverse incentives. A doctor calls the station nurse and says, "I want to admit a patient. Do you have a bed?" The nurse knows that if she says yes, she'll have a ton of extra work to do. It's much more to her advantage to say, "I'm sorry; we're really pretty full today." Then she can get out the door on time at the end of her shift.

When I supervised a group of medical transcriptionists, I paid them by the word. However many words they keyed into the computer was multiplied by a fixed rate, and that's how much they earned. This group got into a fight at one point about phone duty. Nobody wanted to answer questions that might be called into the department because that meant time away from keying.

So I said, "OK, I'll pay you by the hour instead." All of a sudden, they were willing to field phone calls because it meant getting a break from the drudgery of typing. Productivity took a plunge.

These were the same people as before—the "same bear," if you will. Only the rewards of the performance system had changed.

Children and teenagers experience systems that backfire all the time. An old Calvin and Hobbes cartoon is a good example:

Calvin: "I got expelled from school again."

Hobbes: "Why did they kick you out?"

Calvin: "Because I hit somebody."

Hobbes: "Why did you hit him?"

Calvin: "So I could get three days off from school."

A junior-higher mouths off at the evening dinner table. "Go to your room!" says the upset parent. The kid readily gets up from the table (stuffing an extra roll in his mouth as he does) and heads down the hall. He's not that bothered. Why? Because his room has a PlayStation waiting.

The kid is being conditioned opposite of what the parent truly wants. He's thinking, *If I don't like sitting here with my sisters, I can just say something rude, and I'll get a quick pass to go do something more fun.*

Without realizing it, we have reward systems for doing the wrong thing and punishment systems for doing the right thing! How crazy is that?

Intelligent Design

The great challenge for all adults who have responsibility for difficult young people is to think through the performance system *from the kid's point of view* and then make adjustments. These may be slight rather than dramatic; that's OK. They can still get to a tipping point where the incentive to do right starts outweighing the incentive to keep doing wrong.

To visualize this, think of a traditional balance scale.

Doing the Wrong Thing   **Doing the Right Thing**

On a scale of 1 to 10 . . .

BENEFITS	Weight		BENEFITS	Weight
_____	+ ____		_____	+ ____
_____	+ ____		_____	+ ____
_____	+ ____		_____	+ ____
CONSEQUENCES	Weight		CONSEQUENCES	Weight
_____	- ____		_____	- ____
_____	- ____		_____	- ____
_____	- ____		_____	- ____
TOTAL for doing wrong ____			**TOTAL for doing right** ____	

One end of the bar represents "If I do the wrong thing . . ." and has both rewards and consequences. The other end represents "If I do the right thing . . ." and also has rewards and consequences. The entire goal is to tip the bar from negative behavior to positive behavior, even if ever so gradually. A quarter of an inch is good enough.

Let's use the example of a fourteen-year-old boy smoking marijuana. How does the scale look from where *he* stands (not where we stand)? See the diagram below.

Doing the Wrong Thing   **Doing the Right Thing**

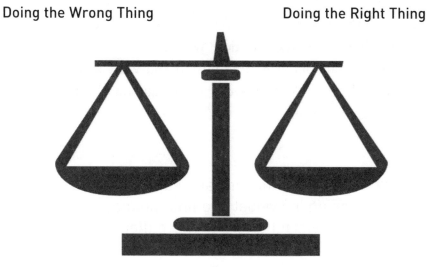

On a scale of 1 to 10 . . .

BENEFITS	Weight	BENEFITS	Weight
High feels good	+8	Parents would be proud	+3
Friends think I'm cool	+9	Higher self-esteem	+3
I feel all mature, in charge	+6	Better health in the future?	+1

CONSEQUENCES	Weight	CONSEQUENCES	Weight
Mom/Dad yell at me	-4	Friends would laugh at me	-10
If I got caught, I'd go to jail	-2	I'd miss the high	-5
Health problem in 50 years?	-1	I'd feel like a "little kid"	-7
TOTAL for doing wrong	**+16**	**TOTAL for doing right**	**-15**

It doesn't take much analysis to see that to this fourteen-year-old the left side is more attractive than the right. It's a classic case of good deeds getting punished, as far as the fourteen-year-old is concerned. No wonder the kid opts to keep smoking pot.

What is a parent or guardian to do in this situation? How can the scale be tipped? Which of the four tools will be effective?

One method is to make the negative consequences, which are currently quite vague, be more realistic. Someone in the legal profession can talk about getting busted and what it does to your scholarship chances. A doctor can shed light on the true health ramifications of marijuana.

> We have to understand each person
> as an individual and find the most
> powerful levers to move them.

At the same time, a parent could say, "How about if we do random UAs (urine analyses), and every time you pass, you get a money reward from me?" Granted, that's not the most noble reason for saying no to drugs, but it's better than ongoing usage, right?

Another approach: "Every time you come home and tell me a true story about how you said no to drugs, I'll put a towel over my arm and be your butler for an hour! Any service you want, from a soda with ice to a back rub—just ask!" This injects some humor into what is otherwise a very heavy subject, and it builds relationship.

These are just a few ways to adjust the scale so that the benefits of saying no start to grow, eventually outweighing the pleasures of saying yes.

Each young person is different. This can't be a cookie-cutter strategy. Some fourteen-year-olds will be moved by money while others couldn't care less; they want social approval. If, on the consequences side, you take away one boy's basketball, he'll be crushed. The next boy will hardly notice. We have to understand each person as an individual, know what makes them tick, and find the most powerful levers so they get more out of doing the right thing than doing the wrong thing.

Naturally, it helps if the kid comes into adolescence with a built-in moral code from earlier teaching. If the boy carries a belief that God created the human body and doesn't approve of messing it up with harmful substances, then that's a strong weight on the consequence scale. But if he's never been instructed that way, he won't care what God thinks. The individual's value system makes a big difference here.

A different example: What about the sophomore girl who's sleeping around? What are the benefits as far as she's concerned, and why are they stronger than the consequences?

For most girls, the main reward is more social acceptance than physical pleasure. She likes the fact that her boyfriend "loves" her (at least that's what he says). Her girlfriends think she's really daring and grown up. She's living the life she reads about in the magazines. All this is worth more than the disapproval of older adults, or God.

Kids do this kind of cost-benefit analysis in their heads all the time. It's a feedback loop that happens almost subconsciously. We have to ask how we might socially reengineer the girl's world so that there's more stigma to loose sex than there is reward.

Most girls in this situation, I've found, have narrowed their range of social acquaintances down to a small group of people who agree with them. They are almost in a cult that rewards negative behavior.

It won't work to say flatly, "Don't hang around with those people." Instead, we have to expand the social group to create some disharmony, some alternate opinions. It may be a sports team, a cousin who's living morally, or an attractive church youth group—anybody who will say, at the opportune moment, "You're doing what? That doesn't make a lot of sense."

One of the best ways to get a person out of a problematic relationship is to steer them toward another relationship that doesn't mesh. The conflicting values cause reassessment.

Simultaneously, you might invite a teen girl who has a baby to come over to your house for dinner some weekend. Let your daughter see how much work a baby can be, how loud it cries, and how constrained the teen mother's life has become in terms of both time and money. This again sends a dissonant message about sexual activity.

In the area of *giving something good,* you can increase the opportunities to do fun things that don't lead to time alone with a guy. A girl who's busy with lots of positive activities is less likely to offer herself to premature intimacy.

These are small interventions, to be sure. They may not look like much on the surface, but they can add up over time to tipping the scale. The benefits of doing the right thing start to build up, and behavior changes.

> Small interventions may not
> look like much on the surface,
> but they can add up over time.

Even when kids do the right thing for the wrong reason—for example, because they've been bribed—it starts to internalize the desired result. The neural patterns that have been formed in the past get rerouted. Eventually, the new behavior becomes a habit.

This isn't as dramatic as a sudden "moment of truth" that we all wish for. We'd like to see the light dawn in a kid's mind, triggering a 180-degree turn overnight. I am all in favor of miracles, believe me! But I've noticed over the years that it's more often a process than an event. The unhealthy behavior is extinguished over time as the positive behavior is reinforced—all because we adjusted the performance system.

The Girl Who Majored in Sleep

We once had a fifteen-year-old foster girl in our agency named Chelsea. She was sophisticated enough to analyze that if she made life bad enough for every home in which she was placed, she might get us all to give up on her and put her back with her drug-addicted mom. This led to a strategy of passive resistance.

At the time, her foster parents were in their mid thirties, and Sharon was a delightful woman who wanted to do all kinds of fun things with Chelsea. She bought her ice skates; she scanned the newspaper for weekend events; she tried her best to enliven Chelsea's life.

Chelsea, on the other hand, would do nothing but sleep. By the end of the first month, she was refusing to go to school. She wouldn't talk to the family members. She wouldn't even get dressed. She insisted on just hiding in her room.

The school would call to check on her truancy. Sharon was frustrated, not knowing what to say. Chelsea got suspended—which was of course, just fine with her. She was sabotaging the whole arrangement.

"Ross, I don't think we can keep her," Sharon said to me one day, "because we can't engage her. *We can't get her to do anything.* She's just this lump lying in her room. I'm worried—do you think she's suicidal? Help!"

At her caseworker appointments, Chelsea would say, "Yeah, I know. I must be a horrible, awful kid. You ought to just kick me out and send me home." At least she was forthright about her goal!

The psychiatrist talked about maybe changing her medications. The only trouble was, she wasn't even taking her meds anymore. She was basically winning on every point. She had all the professionals standing around scratching their heads, and she was loving every minute of it.

At this point I got together with Sharon, her husband, and the others and pulled out a piece of paper. "OK," I said, "let's analyze the performance system. What is Chelsea getting positively for doing the wrong things? She's getting a lot of attention. She's got everybody worked up. She's also enjoying a life of leisure." People started laughing and saying, "Hey, I could go for that kind of life myself!"

"She also thinks," I added, "that she's making headway toward her goal, which is getting back to her mom."

Then I asked what were the current consequences of doing the wrong thing. We had to admit there were none. We couldn't think of much to take away from her except the roof over her head, which was what she wanted.

We then moved to the right side of the paper. What were the rewards for doing the right thing? Interaction and fun with others . . . a diploma . . . a chance at a decent job later on. None of those would cut any ice with Chelsea, we knew. She would just say she could have all those things by getting back to her mom.

What were the consequences or downsides of doing the right thing? Here we hit pay dirt. The consequence, in her distorted mind, of coming out of her shell and cooperating with foster care was that she would lose her mom. She'd never get back home again.

"We see this in foster care all the time, don't we?" I said to the group. "The kid thinks that if he accepts his foster dad, he's betraying his real dad. Belonging here means forfeiting membership over there."

Out of this discussion came several action points.

First we decided to cut down the rewards for doing wrong by cutting off all the flurry of attention. Sharon was instructed to go home and say, "Guess what, Chelsea? You've won. The tug-of-war is over. You can stay in your room as long as you like. I'm calling the school and disenrolling you. I'm telling them not to expect you to come to school. They'll think we're enrolling you somewhere else so they'll leave you alone.

"I'm calling your therapist and getting you officially discharged as a patient. No more hassle from him. You can just veg in your room as much as you want."

This, as it turned out, was a little disconcerting to Chelsea. She saw the "system" getting comfortable with her after all. Nobody was going to be churned up over her. That wasn't what she had in mind.

Meanwhile, Sharon continued, "By the way, don't feel any obligation to come upstairs where the rest of us are. We'll be there, and we'd enjoy having you around because you're a great kid—but no pressure, you understand. It's your call. Anytime you feel like showing up, come ahead. But if we don't see you for a day or two or three, that's OK.

"As for bringing food down to you: no, I don't think so anymore. You're not going to starve. If you want food, come on up and get it. If not, hey, it's up to you."

Chelsea was once again thrown off-balance.

This covered the removal of benefits for her withdrawal. Next came some consequences. "The allowance you've been getting? Well, that won't be happening anymore because it's tied to the chores that you do—and I'm not going to bug you about those, OK? And the fun things we've done are basically over. If you don't go to school during the day, then you can't do activities with us in the evenings. Just thought you'd want to know."

What about benefits for doing the right thing? We instructed Sharon that if Chelsea ever did venture upstairs, she should flip out with joy. "Hey! Cool! Great to see you! I wasn't going to interrupt you if you were sleeping, but since you're here, I could really use your help moving this table to the other side of the kitchen. Can you give me a hand? . . . I've been trying to figure out this crossword puzzle, and I'm stuck. What's a five-letter word ending with R that means 'stream or tributary'?"

Finally we got to the heavy quadrant: consequence for doing the right thing, which was huge in her mind. She believed this would be betraying her mother.

We arranged for her mom to show up one day. Sharon called down the stairs, "Hey, Chelsea! We have a visitor you might want to meet."

"Who is it?"

"It's your mom. If you want to come up and meet her, that would be great. But if you want to stay downstairs in your room, that's OK, too. . . ."

Boom! Chelsea was upstairs in a flash. There she ran to grab her mother in a big hug, of course. As soon as she let go, however, she saw that her caseworker had also come along. A short meeting ensued.

Chelsea was informed that two things had to happen in order for her to get back with her mom. First, Mom had to succeed in her drug rehab program; and second, Chelsea had to succeed in foster care. "That's the only way you guys can be with each other. You will never go back to your mom as long as you're not making it in foster care. Just thought you'd want to know what the playing field is," the caseworker announced.

This proved to be the kicker. Chelsea realized that her two moms were working together. "Honey, it really makes me upset that you're not being very nice to Sharon and her husband," the mom said. "We have to see this through, both of us."

> When Chelsea realized that her two moms were working together, she began to participate with the family.

Right away Chelsea began to participate with the family. This wasn't a betrayal of her birth mom after all. This was, in fact, the way back. She even asked to be enrolled in school again. That was tough to manage, of course, since she had fallen so far behind. The educational system would have slammed her with an avalanche of Ds and Fs had we not pled for amnesty. "Please don't flunk her right away," we said. "Just give her incompletes, OK? We need time to restart the learning engines here."

Chelsea ended up going the GED route to a high school diploma. She is out of foster care today, taking care of herself as a young adult. Reorganizing the performance system by giving attention to all four areas on her scale made all the difference.

Yes, it sounds like a manipulative game. But the truth is, we simply adjusted the feedback loops. We altered reality enough for her to see a different road to her goals. Her scale tipped to the other side after all.

Taming the Tiger

Let me share one more story that is opposite in some ways. Instead of dealing with a phlegmatic girl, it's about an aggressive, even violent, boy and his siblings.

Joseph was only nine years old, but he was big for his age—you could have mistaken him for twelve. He and his two little sisters, ages six and three, were in foster care because their dad, a construction worker, was extremely violent; he had almost killed one of the girls and would soon be going to prison. Their mom, unfortunately, was what a psychiatrist would term "nonprotective," a woman so passive she would just stand by and let her husband wale on the kids. She couldn't set any kind of limit or intervention.

Joseph, unfortunately, had learned a lot from his father. He saw himself as the big bad authority now, the "man of the house" since Dad had been removed. He carried a grudge against his sister, in fact—the one who had almost died at their father's hand—because "that's what started all this trouble" that resulted in the loss of Dad. Joseph was generally mad at the world and ready to straighten it out with his fists.

I'll never forget the day the children were brought to our brand-new visitation center to see Mom. We had just opened up this nice room with couches and toys to accommodate hour-long, supervised visits with birth parents. A new staff member with her master's degree in childhood education—her name was Micah—was assigned to oversee the meeting.

Mom was glad to see her kids, of course. Everything went well until it was time to leave. Joseph, not wanting to go back to the foster home, pitched a fit. He started throwing chairs, pushing people, jumping up and down on the couch, and yelling threats. "You can't make me! I ain't goin'! I'm staying with my mom!"

Trying to defuse the tension, Micah suggested to Mom that she go on out to her car first. Then Micah bent down to Joseph's level to try to explain in a calm voice that Mommy really did need to go now, but there would be another visit soon—

Thwack! Joseph reeled back and landed a solid punch right into Micah's nose. Her graduate school courses somehow had not led her to expect this, for sure. Within sixty seconds I got word up in my office that the visitation room had erupted, furniture was being thrown, and Micah was fighting back the tears.

By the time I ran down the stairs, Joseph had apparently realized he had crossed some kind of line. He was headed out the door toward the foster parents' car after all. I went to console my staff member. "Micah, I'm so sorry! What happened? Is your nose broken?" We gathered around to examine her closely and see whether she needed to go to the emergency room. Her nose seemed intact after all.

As she regained her composure, someone called the county caseworker, who said, "We'll definitely make sure this doesn't happen again." Visitation next week would surely go better, we hoped.

The caseworker came along the following week to help Micah hold the fort. Mom showed up again, the kids were glad to see her, and another pleasant visit ensued. Until farewell time, that is.

I glanced out my office window toward the parking lot, only to see the foster dad and the caseworker struggling with all their combined might to get Joseph into the car, kicking and screaming. The two little girls were already inside. I realized as I ran to help that the sequence had been reversed this week; the kids had been excused first, while their mother remained in the building a few extra minutes. Joseph was ferociously determined to get back to his mother.

The foster dad happened to be African-American, and Joseph was shouting the N-word and every other racial slur he could think of as he fought for his freedom. He kicked the man in the shins, then sank his teeth into the man's forearm, leaving large gashes. The pain jolted the foster dad enough that he lost his grip on Joseph, who grabbed his littlest sister out of the car and started running with her toward Lake Avenue, a major four-lane highway at the bottom of the hill.

I went running down the slope and managed to grab the three-year-old before she got into the traffic. "Here, take her back!" I yelled to the caseworker, who was right behind me. I then turned to Joseph, who continued yelling and swinging his fists wildly in my direction. I ducked, he missed a couple of times—but then he made his mark by unleashing the biggest wad of spit he could muster right into my face. His aim this time was perfect.

The caseworker soon came back to help, and the two of us grabbed enough arms and legs to get Joseph off the boulevard and back up to the parking lot. By now his steam was starting to fade. He reluctantly got into the car but kept screaming as we sent him on his way home.

The mother was mortified, of course. "I'm so sorry, I'm so sorry," she kept repeating with a heavy sigh. "I don't know what to do with these kids. . . ."

Well, we knew *we* had better figure out what to do with these kids before the third visit came around. If we didn't, we'd no doubt lose Micah, having just hired her. You could tell she pretty much hated her job so far.

On the morning of the next visitation day, I pulled Micah aside. "Are you looking forward to Joseph and his sisters coming today?" I asked with feigned innocence.

Her eyes drooped.

"OK, I'm going to tell you the secret to make this a great visit," I said. "You're going to have to trust me on this one. Here's a twenty-dollar bill. I want you to run down to the discount toy store and buy three presents for those kids. Not an individual present for each child, but three things that all three can enjoy together. Wrap them up and have them ready for the visitation."

Micah looked at me like I was dreaming. But she did as instructed.

When the mom arrived four hours later, I pulled her aside and briefed her on what would be happening. I gave her some lines to say at certain times. She, being the super-compliant person she was, meekly agreed to follow my orders.

Meanwhile, one wrapped present was stashed in a cabinet in the visitation room. The second and third were secreted into the foster family's car once the kids were inside the building.

I opened the session this third week by saying, "Now, Joseph, I realize that you get really upset when you don't get to spend time with your mom. That's hard, I know. But here's the deal: since you're the oldest kid here, and you're kind of in charge, I want you to realize that future visits with your mom are under your control. If you blow up like you did last time, you won't be coming back to this visitation center again. Your caseworker will have to find some other visitation place for you guys—and who knows what their rules will be. You might even wind up seeing Mom less. So you decide if you want to make this situation work or not. It's up to you."

He looked at me with a serious gaze. I could tell he wondered where I was headed next.

"And another thing: halfway through our visit today, we're going to practice saying good-bye. We'll take a few minutes and go through the motions of saying good-bye and heading out to the cars. If you and the girls do well at this, then we'll go ahead with the second half of the visit. But if it all falls apart, then that's it—we'll cut off the visit right then. You understand what I'm saying, right?"

Joseph nodded. In his head, he clearly saw how to get what he wanted, which was more time with Mom.

We did the mid-visit role play, and it went smoothly. He got his reward. The new neural pathway, which said that *good things follow if I control myself,* was starting to be plowed.

As the clock ticked down to the fateful moment, I said brightly, "Hey, kids, guess what. I think your mom has something special for you."

Mom joined in right on cue. "Yes, I do," she said, smiling. "I have a present for you."

"What? What? What is it?" they all cheered at once.

She pulled the present out of the cabinet. They tore open the wrapping to find a toss-the-beanbag game that all three of them could play at home. "Thank you, Mom!" they cried, giving her warm hugs.

"Now guess what?" she continued. "Down in your foster parents' car, are two more presents waiting for you! If you can walk down there calmly and get into your seats like good kids, I'll come along behind, give you the second present, and kiss each of you good-bye. But if you start yelling and causing trouble, then Mr. Wright says I have to leave right now."

You should have seen Joseph marshalling his little sisters down the steps and out to the car. He ended up, in fact, being the first to get his seat belt latched once they arrived. Here was the way to get what he wanted: more attention from Mom.

She congratulated them on such wonderful behavior and then pulled out the second present. Again there were cries of "Oh, cool! This is neat!" when it was opened. She gave each of the three a kiss and a hug.

Then she pulled out present number three. "I want you to be really good for these folks," she said, nodding toward the foster parents. "When you get home, call me on the phone and tell me you did really great all the ride home, OK? If that is what happens, then you can open this third present while we're on the phone together!"

"Sure, Mom! We'll do it!" they cried. With that the engine started, and off they went.

> Micah looked at me in absolute disbelief. "You've got to be kidding!" she exclaimed.

We had rearranged the performance system.

Standing there in the parking lot, Micah looked at me in absolute disbelief. "You've got to be kidding!" she exclaimed.

"Well, Micah, that's how it works," I replied. "We figure out what the kid considers valuable, and we set up the playing field to push him in an appropriate direction based on his motivations. He's the same kid he's always been. We've just slotted him for success instead of pandemonium."

In subsequent weeks, Joseph turned out to be a star performer. No more presents were needed. He kept seeing that his goal of time with Mom was reachable through civilized behavior. And we kept pumping him up: "Joseph, you're the man here. For your sisters and everybody, it all rides on your shoulders."

We had gotten out of battle mode with him, choosing instead to step back, reorganize the system, and let the consequences that the child accepts just happen to align with our goals.

More than Tips

This matrix is a comprehensive plan for adjusting behavior. It takes some time and forethought to lay the strategy. But once it's in place, the results can be dramatic.

I spoke on this once to a large group of women at my church, and you could just see the lightbulbs coming on. One mother came up afterward to say, "When I go to parenting classes, most of the time it seems that I just come away with little 'tips'—you know, try this or try that with your kid and see if it works. If not, try something else.

"You've given us a whole system here. I can plug in my kid's particular issues, weigh them individually, and see what will motivate him to change. This is so much more substantial."

Four questions lie at the heart of all this:

1. What are the current rewards (to the child) for doing the wrong thing? Make a list. . . .
2. What are the consequences for doing the wrong thing? Make a list. . . .
3. What could be the rewards for doing the right thing? Make a list. . . .
4. What could be the consequences for doing the right thing? Make a list. . . .

Then comes the process of sitting back and analyzing which things on which lists are the most powerful. These tend to dominate the other, weaker elements, and they require more counterbalancing.

Finally, we begin constructing our responses that will end up tipping the scale in the direction we want.

A common proverb that we've all heard says, "Practice makes perfect." No, actually, it doesn't. Practice simply makes *permanent*. It wears the behavior into an ever deeper groove—for good or ill. Ask any golfer who has hacked away for years.

The phrase ought to be, "*Feedback* makes perfect." In the world of music or sports, the teacher or the coach tells us what we're doing awkwardly and how to correct it. We listen and then get busy setting a new groove.

In the world of parenting, the same dynamic is true: A well-designed performance system gives *feedback* to a child, who promptly adjusts his or her "swing" in daily life to be more successful.

Putting the two phrases together, we can say that *"Practice plus feedback make perfection permanent."* As this happens, the batting average for life steadily soars. We find that we are moving our children more and more in the direction of healthy, self-regulating adulthood—which is what we've dreamed of all along.

CHAPTER

9

The Power of Rewards

If *giving a child something good* is the strongest tool we have, as claimed in the previous chapter, then perhaps we ought to examine it more closely. The method is worth understanding to the fullest.

I am aware, however, of an opposite thread in current discussion. Some say rewards are manipulative and they lead nowhere in the end. The Internet is full of this viewpoint. Alfie Kohn, to cite just one example, wrote a book a few years ago entitled *Punished by Rewards: The Trouble with Gold Stars, Incentive Plans, A's, Praise, and Other Bribes.*[1] This Boston author keeps up a busy speaking schedule to educational and business groups on how external considerations, and the competition they engender, are bad for our social health as a nation.

With all due respect, I beg to differ. I have seen too much lasting progress in kids who have been pulled out of negative and self-destructive patterns by well-thought-out rewards. (Also, I couldn't help smiling at one Amazon.com reviewer's question on the Kohn title: "Did he write the book for free? Think about it. . . .") Rewards have a way of nudging us in the right direction, where we can then discover the intrinsic benefits of doing well. We might never know that it's good to keep a clean room or to happily entertain a younger sibling if we had not been coaxed there, at least in the early years, by a payoff of some kind.

Granted, rewards can be abused. They can even tempt us toward harmful activities. "Sign up for this new credit card (at just 48 percent interest), and we'll give you a free travel clock!" But the underlying truth is that we are all wired to respond to incentives, and this basic trait can be used to accomplish much good.

Rewards and Bribes: Not the Same

First of all, let me clarify that a reward is different from a bribe. The word *bribe* refers to a specific kind of payment that moves a person to do what was already contracted to be done (or not done) without specific payment. The police officer took an oath on day one to uphold and defend the traffic laws; he or she should not then have to be paid to come investigate an accident—or to refrain from writing a speeding ticket. The officer made a formal commitment to do the specified job and thereby earn a given salary. No further cash is required. Fortunately, the vast majority of police in this country operate by these rules.

Children, on the other hand, haven't signed any contracts with us to do (or not do) anything. They are still figuring out their role in life. They are still acquiring the proper do's and don'ts of society. They are not our employees. To reward them for doing well is entirely appropriate. It's part of their learning process.

Rewards and incentives comprise a much bigger category than the narrow box called "bribes." These words refer to the wider landscape of influencing another person's behavior for good through external means. How many of us adults would get out of bed Monday morning and go to work if we weren't getting a paycheck every two weeks? We readily expect to be compensated for our labor. It seems a bit hypocritical, then, to expect children to do the right thing solely because "virtue is its own reward."

> How many of us adults would get out of bed Monday morning and go to work if we weren't getting a paycheck every two weeks?

Performance in the workplace is further enhanced by rewards that have nothing to do with money. A good employee gets a plaque, or an up-front parking place for the month. Hopefully, the employee gets verbal praise from the department manager, if not the vice president. One supervisor of an editorial department at a publishing house told me how he incentivized his staff to meet deadlines. "Look," he explained in a staff meeting, "I really wish I had the budget to give you a bonus for hitting the dates on the schedule, but I don't. I'll tell you what I *can* do, however. We'll keep a chart on the wall here for every team. Whenever your particular group makes three monthly deadlines, so that three issues of your magazine get out the door and headed for the printer on time, I'll give everybody in the group a half-day off with pay—in other words, an extra half day of vacation time. Go to the beach or the mountains on a Friday afternoon and enjoy yourself."

The man told me later, "It was amazing how people scurried around to stay on time. Writers and designers, who are creative by nature, can usually come up with all kinds of excuses why the article just didn't get done—but suddenly the excuses dried up. People began actually harassing each other to get moving, wrap up the issue, and be sure they didn't jeopardize everybody's half day off!"

Sometimes adult rewards are downright cheesy. You join an auto club, and they give you a little red, white, and blue sticker to put on your car bumper or window. Why? So you can let everybody know you're part of the in-group. Imagine it: sophisticated adults wanting a sticker!

If this kind of thing works for adults, why not for kids? What is their "work"? Well, from age five on up, a big piece of their assignment in life is school. That's the place they go five days a week with certain expectations of productivity. The rewards take the shape of everything from grades to blue ribbons to trophies to the annual promotion from one grade to the next.

I met one couple who was totally up-front about this with their son and twin daughters. They knew the kids had good aptitude to start with, so they said, "OK, here's the deal: For every A on your report card, you earn five bucks. For every B, you earn three bucks. This is your 'pay' for a job well done. Cs and on down don't get you anything because we know you can do better than that.

"By the way, we're not just talking about the academic subjects. We're interested in the 'citizenship' side of the report card, too, where you get graded for behavior, attitude, etc. So we'll pay for that side of things as well."

The kids were happy to be rewarded for their efforts. This plan no doubt had something to do with the fact that years later, at college commencement ceremonies, all three young people graduated summa cum laude.

Another woman I met did the same thing, only with a twist: She said she would pay a *hundred* dollars for every A and *fifty* dollars for every B, provided the payments went into savings bonds for college. At the end of every semester, she and her daughter would go down to the bank and buy five or six savings bonds. (The cash outlay, of course, was only half the face amount of the bond: fifty dollars for an A, twenty-five for a B.)

The daughter watched excitedly as the stack of savings bonds grew thick over time. The mom told me, "I figured I was going to have to pay for college anyway, so I might as well get some mileage out of it here in the early years. Plus, this program disciplined me to start saving for college in advance rather than stalling until later.

"But the best part was the message it implanted in my daughter's head: *I'm valuable. I'm special. I'm going to college. See, my mom's already planning ahead for that. Doing well in school today has a connection to college tomorrow.*"

Perhaps the reason rewards seem so natural to us is that the idea traces all the way back to the Creator. The ancient book of Proverbs says, "He who is kind to the poor lends to the Lord, and he will reward him for what he has done" (19:17). When I read that verse, I think about some of our foster families pouring their lives into kids from desperately deprived environments. I can't help imagining the big reward that awaits them down the line.

Jesus talked openly in the Sermon on the Mount about private giving, praying, and fasting, saying all three times, "Then your Father, who sees what is done in secret, will reward you" (Matt. 6:4, 6, 18). The apostle Paul wrote about a future day when every person's "work will be shown for what it is, because the Day will bring it to light. . . . If what he has built survives, he will receive his reward" (1 Cor. 3:13–14). God apparently has an extensive reward system in place, with results to be announced at the end of time.

Rewards, if handled properly, can make a huge difference in a young person's life. Here are six things I've learned that build effectiveness:

1. Keep rewards simple.

Too often we adults get carried away when planning rewards, winding up with elaborate ideas we can't afford anyway. Meanwhile, the little child needs nothing more than a pat on the back, a smile, or a chance to choose the supper menu. I've never forgotten a handbook to Disneyland I saw that included a warning for parents of young children. It frankly admitted that the theme park may be too much, too overwhelming for a child that age. It told of a survey of children under seven:

Question: "What was your most favorite thing about your trip to Disneyland?"

Most popular answer: "Playing in the hotel pool with my dad."

That pretty much says it all. Kids, especially young kids, don't need big, expensive rewards nearly as much as they need the warm and loving touch of a caring parent. They don't want things as much as they want *us.*

2. Keep rewards relational whenever possible.

Closely related to the first point is this one: Figure out ways to enjoy the reward *together* if you can. "Hey, when we get done with this job, how about if you and I take the dogs for a walk?" "This math paper from school looks really good, Daniel. Wanna shoot some baskets down at the park?"

Notice, these kinds of rewards don't cost a dime. But they pay amazing dividends in enriching the parent-child relationship. The child senses that he or she is valued.

My wife, who works alongside me in the agency, got a call not long ago from a foster mom on the edge of tears. The three kids in her home (ranging from age six to twelve) were making life miserable. Nothing was going right. The oldest one especially was leading the way in provoking and taunting.

"How about if you all come in for a talk tomorrow morning?" Bridgette said.

> Young kids don't need big, expensive rewards nearly as much as they need the warm and loving touch of a caring parent.

When they sat down together, the conversation quickly launched into what all the boys were doing badly and how frustrated the foster mom was. Bridgette listened for awhile and then interrupted with something totally off the wall.

"Hey, have you guys ever been to Mr. Biggs?" (That's the name of a family amusement center in our city, with everything from miniature golf to go-carts to laser tag.)

No, nobody had been there.

Bridgette whipped out some flyers to whet their appetite. "I'll tell you what," she continued. "On the way home today, you drive by the place and just take a look. Then I'm going to give your house a call in a week. If your foster mom says you've had a good week at home, I'll come by on Saturday, and we'll all go to Mr. Biggs together. How's that?"

Everybody thought that was a cool idea. When Bridgette called the next Friday, the report was mixed: the boys' behavior had improved somewhat, but not good enough to warrant the reward.

They had their eye on the goal by now, however; they immediately began talking among themselves about how to behave better. A trip to Mr. Biggs had become the guiding star. By the second week they had earned their outing after all, to the delight of everyone involved.

Call it bribery if you want, but I prefer to see what Bridgette did as a calculated intervention. She disrupted the negative pattern of behavior with the promise of an excursion, thereby resetting the landscape. The entry tickets were a small price to pay for getting the boys onto a better footing.

I'm not saying it solved their issues forever. It simply bought a week in which to groove new habits of speech and conduct.

3. *Choose rewards according to the* child's *criteria, not yours.*

This one should be obvious—except that we adults sometimes forget. I have seen more than a few occasions in which parents thought they were giving a reward and the child thought he was being punished. I admit I've even done it myself. Being an American history buff, I thought I was being a great dad the day on vacation in San Francisco when I dragged my family through a fascinating submarine, the *USS Pampanito.* The displays were incredible, and the story of how this ship fought in the Pacific during World War II, sinking six Japanese vessels, was riveting . . . to me, that is. The rest of the family only got seasick and claustrophobic. They certainly did not feel rewarded for anything.

Sometimes the reverse is true: What feels like a reward to the child is a punishment to the parent. So be it. If your twelve-year-old daughter has done something admirable and would like to be affirmed with a four-hour trip to the mall, don't say no. It may be purgatory for you, Dad, but keep quiet. The point is to reinforce *her* positive behavior. Whatever gets the job done is what you need to facilitate.

4. Don't hit and miss. Be consistent.

This mistake is even easier to make in our hectic contemporary lifestyles. We celebrate one achievement with grand enthusiasm only to draw a blank the next time it happens. The child is left wondering, "What happened? Did I do something wrong? How come they didn't go nuts over this report card like they did last time?"

The psychological term for this is *intermittent rewards*. The confusion in the child's mind turns out, in fact, to be more powerful than the reward itself. They don't know if their work is going to be noticed or not. They start to shut down.

In fact, it can sometimes get even worse than that. They can start acting like the mice in one study that psychologists ran. First the mice were put into a chute with two buttons to push at the far end. The button on one side gave them food while the other button released a trap door that dropped them into a tray of water—something that all mice hate.

Now mice are quick at conditioning, so it didn't take long before these mice figured out the system. Within two or three tries, they would run down the chute and push the food button every time.

Then the scientists began messing with their heads. They started switching the hidden connections so that the food button would sometimes release the trap door, and the trap door button would sometimes give them food. Or sometimes only one button would work, while the other would be dead. The mice never knew what to expect.

What was the result? You would think the mice would just freeze altogether.

Not so. Time and again the mice would run down the chute and voluntarily throw themselves over the edge into the water, without even pushing a button. Better to accept the bad news and get it over with, they seemed to think, than to endure the anxiety of not knowing what was going to happen. That sounds crazy, but it is absolutely what happened in the experiment. The mice would deliberately choose what they hated in order to resolve the ambiguity.

I have seen children do the same thing. If they're not sure what kind of reaction adults are going to give them, they deliberately act out, provoking Mom or Dad to lose their temper, so as to get the explosion over with. Even kids who are right on the edge of some success will sabotage their own efforts if they are ambiguous about getting a reward for it. Why would they do such a self-defeating thing? Because they've been down the failure road many times in the past, and at least it is a known factor. *I might as well stick to what I'm familiar with,* they tell themselves, *rather than risk a fresh disappointment.*

Counselors find that even adults do this in certain cases, such as domestic violence. If, say, a husband has a history of hitting his wife, the couple realizes after a while that a build-up phase usually precedes it. Things keep getting more and more tense, the pressure in the pressure cooker keeps rising over a period of days, until the man finally lashes out. The crazy thing is, the woman who senses this buildup and can tell the gauge is almost to its peak will sometimes deliberately trigger it by a sarcastic word or other action—just to get it over with. The anxiety of not knowing when he's going to strike is worse than just bringing it on and taking your lumps now.

The term for this is *learned helplessness.* The adult or child in such a predicament says to himself or herself, *I'm helpless here. Whatever I do, I don't know if it's going to improve matters or make them worse. Sometimes I do the right thing, and I get a big hug. The next time, I get ignored. Once in a while I even get slammed up against the wall. So, whatever. . . .*

And some even go so far as to conclude, *I might as well go hit the wall on my own—at least I'll know where I stand. I will reject them before they reject me.*

Obviously, whatever positive rewards we promise a child have to be delivered promptly. We must stay consistent. The child has to know that if he or she does a good job, it is definitely going to be noticed and applauded. Every time—no matter how busy we get with other responsibilities and distractions in our life.

5. *But don't get in a rut. Supplement with spontaneity.*

On the other hand, it's not a good idea for the reward to stay the same year in and year out. Kids love to be surprised. Within the context of consistent reward policy that makes sure to reinforce positive behavior, variety can be the spice of life.

And additional, out-of-the-blue rewards are valuable too. Coming up with a special treat when it is *not* report card week is a brilliant move. The parent says, "Hey, I've been thinking about you all day long. You've done such a good job with keeping your room straight the last couple of weeks. Let's go get that summer swimsuit you've been wanting. Let's go right now! You're terrific."

Kids go nuts over this kind of thing. Our action supercharges the performance system. The kid gets jazzed to see us being spontaneous for once in our orderly, dutiful lives. A party atmosphere takes over for a couple of hours.

It's like when the boss walks up to your desk and says, "You've really been hitting it hard the last month, I know. I appreciate your extra effort. Here's a gift certificate—take your wife (or husband) out to dinner this weekend." We can't wipe the grin off our face for the rest of the day.

Kids are the same way. Every so often, they need to be caught off guard with a surprise reward. They will, as a result, work all the harder for the next scheduled evaluation.

6. *Don't ever ever ever give a negative reward.*

Who would do such a terrible thing, you ask? Mainly parents who simply aren't paying attention. They come home from work exhausted.

They've had a really hard day. The traffic was a hassle. And just then their kid comes running into the kitchen waving a paper from school. "Look! Look! Look! Mom, can this go on the refrigerator? It's really cool!" In the process he trips over the dog and lurches against the counter, which knocks over a carton of milk that had just been opened in preparation for the evening meal.

"For heaven's sake, Daniel! Would you watch where you're going? Look at this mess you made! Knock it off."

That's all it takes to send a message to the boy: *Just never mind. She's not interested in my stuff. Stay out of her way.* His positive effort brought a negative reward.

At other times, a parent may promise, say, a Friday night trip to the movies if the child performs up to a certain level. The child succeeds, Friday night arrives, but Dad says, "I'm too tired. How about next week instead?" Or worse yet, Dad forgets to reserve the night on his calendar since the child's performance was not guaranteed at the beginning of the week. He now has a meeting to attend. The child slinks away utterly deflated.

For some children in our world, Friday night arrives, and the parent is not sober. The idea of spending time together would be an embarrassment rather than a reward.

In all these cases, the child loses faith in the performance system. He or she starts to disengage. Working hard is no longer worth it because the promised results don't come to pass. In fact, they often backfire.

Getting the Picture

One of the most powerful examples I know of *giving something good* and seeing great results occurred by total surprise to a foster couple named Charles and Patty. They had accepted two brothers, ages nine and six, and had fallen in love with them to the point of moving toward formal adoption. We were all excited that these boys would have a permanent home and family.

Adoption is a lengthy legal process, of course, that requires months of paperwork, home inspection by the county officials, and so forth. The longer this process went on, however, Charles and Patty began to notice a deterioration in the boys' behavior. They seemed to get into more fights with each other, and the tension in the home kept increasing. The couple began wondering if they were really doing the right thing after all.

Both boys were in therapy at the time, and so this problem was discussed with the psychiatrist. He decided to put them on medication. Even that didn't help. Behavior seemed to worsen with every passing week.

And then one day, all of a sudden . . . the sunshine came out again. The boys were laughing, playing happily with each other, and getting cozy with their foster parents like old times. *What's this all about?* Charles and Patty wondered. *Is this some kind of fluke?*

Ten days later, the boys were still in a good mood. I spoke with the parents at about the three-week mark. They were still shaking their heads.

> If the child loses faith in the performance system, he or she starts to disengage. Working hard is no longer worth it.

"Did you change their diet?" I asked. "Less sugar, perhaps?" No, they couldn't think of any alteration in food.

"What else did you do differently? Think back to that point in time." They couldn't come up with a thing.

Finally, I said, "Let me see your checkbook. Sometimes that reminds people of certain events."

There, in the ledger at about the three-week mark, I found an entry: *Sears Photo Studio—$42.87.* "What was that?" I asked.

"We went in for a family picture," they explained. "It turned out really great—us and the boys. In fact, we bought one of the big sizes, got a nice frame, and put it up on our mantle."

That turned out to be the mystery trigger. The portrait was the silent symbol to the boys that this adoption really was not going to fall apart. They were going to be safe in this home after all. They could finally relax.

What Charles and Patty didn't know was that the boys had previously been with another couple who was seriously moving toward adopting them but then decided they couldn't handle the younger one's behavior. The older brother had taken upon himself the job of keeping his little brother from messing things up this time. He would corner him in the bathroom and preach, "Don't cry. Don't make a big deal out of stuff. Don't make them upset. We have to be good."

This only increased the tension between the two of them. The closer the adoption date came, the more the older guy rode his little brother to stay in line, not to cause trouble, not to mess up . . . which only created more backlash.

And then, all of a sudden one day—the family photo went up over the fireplace. The message hit both boys like a gust of warm air: *We're in! This is a done deal. They're really going to keep us after all. We don't have to be scared anymore.* Every time they would walk through the family room, they would look at that picture and receive reinforcement.

They started telling all their friends at school and in the neighborhood about the upcoming day in family court. "We're going to be adopted on October 22. Our last name is going to change to Schneider. This is where we're going to be from now on. Really!"

Rewards are sometimes different from what we assume. They don't have to be the expensive trip to Six Flags. They can be as simple as playing together in the local swimming pool. They can be as silent as going for a family photo shoot. Whatever their format or price tag, they tell the child a most powerful message: "Ya done good, kid. I'm proud of you. I like you. In fact, I love you. You're going to do OK in life. And I'll be here to stand behind you every day."

10

Four Resolves

If you bring your children on vacation to beautiful Colorado, where I live, you'll probably wind up in one or more tourist shops that offer "panning for gold"! Your kids will soon be begging you to spend six dollars on a bucket of sand that just *might* have a valuable nugget or two, like in the olden days of the gold rush. You'll go outside to a sloping wooden sluice with running water where your child can wash away the sand and see what treasures emerge. (Thank you, ladies and gentlemen, for supporting our state's tourism industry.)

We are often tempted to read books with a similar mentality. We're looking for one or two gems that might apply to our lives while the rest of the content can wash on down the drain. If we come away with a couple of miscellaneous ideas we can use, we say we've gotten our money's worth. Many people even read the Bible this way. They're looking for one-liners to prove a point they already hold, rather than taking in the full sweep of God's truth.

The book you hold in your hands is certainly not a work of divine inspiration like the Bible. But it does offer a comprehensive view on understanding and nurturing the tough kid who has spun out of control. It lays out a blueprint for developing *a self-regulating adult,* the kind of young person who can make wise decisions much of the time—and can see the error of his choices when he doesn't. The child is no longer flailing around in limbo. He or she is instead plotting intelligent steps to get from here to there, whether in building a career, forming a marriage, developing a skill, or facing any other challenge of adult living.

The thrust of all that has been said up to this point distills down to four main decisions on our part:

1. I resolve to keep *showing love* on a regular basis in ways that match my child's developmental stage—no matter how upset I may be at the moment.
2. I resolve to work with my child toward the ends (the *teleo*) that we select together (goal agreement), based on how he/she was created in the first place.
3. I resolve to keep looking for *avenues of achievement* that befit this particular child.
4. I resolve to *reward* positive behaviors and discourage negative ones through a tailor-made performance system until the balance scale tilts the right way.

An easy way to remember this overall structure is the acronym STAR:

S – Showing love

T – Teleology

A – Avenues of achievement

R – Rewards

These actions are not sequential; we don't finish *S* completely, then move along to *T*, to be followed by *A*, and finally *R*. Instead, we are busily engaged with all four all the time. They are like the pistons of a four-cylinder engine, constantly pumping up and down to create the torque that moves the car down the road.

I can almost guarantee that if you pursue these four resolves with even the most troubled young person, you will see ongoing results. You will steadily make headway in the direction of producing a young person who can function normally in life.

In the Crisis

Yes, it's hard to keep the big strategy in mind when you're upset. Your kid comes home from school and, instead of taking his backpack to his room as you've clearly instructed, drops it instead with a thud in the middle of the living room floor. A purple marking pen silently cracks upon impact, leaking ink through the canvas and into the carpet. Two hours later, you come home from work to find a four-inch circle of ink stain in the beige carpet.

Your first instinct is *not* to implement some fine-sounding four-point strategy you read in a book somewhere. This is no time for psychobabble. Instead, you tell yourself the kid is *gonna get it right now*. "Aaron, get yourself in here this very minute!" you screech. You start revving up how many times the storage of backpacks has been discussed in the past, and now the living room is ruined, and you simply cannot believe what a stupid . . . etc., etc.

The trouble with this entirely understandable reaction is that it sends a message to Aaron that says, *My mom cares more about the carpet than she does about me.* That is patently untrue, of course. But in the heat of the moment, such a conclusion is likely. That isn't what you want to convey at all.

> Modest affirmation brings stability
> to a child who was feeling wretched
> about himself. It assures him that
> life will go on after all.

If possible, despite the raging emotions, the child could greatly benefit from a parent who takes a deep breath and then decides to *show love*—even in this ugly situation. It means taking the focus off your personal exasperation and turning instead to what your son truly needs in this moment. Maybe it's a hug. Maybe it's simply the opportunity to see your tears. Maybe it's something as generous as "I know you didn't mean for this to happen"—which is, after all, true.

If you can make it this far, your brain can proceed next to *T* (teleology). You say to yourself, OK, *what's the goal here? What are we trying to get done?* Quickly two items spring to mind: (1) get the spot out somehow, and (2) prevent this kind of thing from ever happening again. Both parent and child can agree on these goals.

A third goal, of course, is to model how a mature human being deals with this kind of event. You want your child to catch a lesson on self-control here.

Soon you move along to *A* (avenues of achievement). "Let's find out if we can get the stain out by ourselves, or are we going to have to call in the professionals," you say. Does your child have a bent toward researching things? Then you might have him call a stain hotline or jump on the Internet in order to find one. Is your child more hands-on? Then you put him to work down on his knees with paper towels trying to sop up whatever ink hasn't yet fully dried. If the experts advise you that the purple blotch is impossible to remove, maybe the two of you go crawling up in the attic to see if you still have remnants that a carpet layer could use as a square patch.

In all of these, you're focusing *together* on a possible *solution* rather than just fuming about the initial damage.

Eventually, you come to *R* (rewards), which sounds preposterous, I know. You certainly don't want to reward a kid for carelessness that wrecked the carpet. But the fact is, his emotional piggy bank is empty. He needs *some* kind of deposit to let him know he's not totally despicable. Something along the lines of "Wow, this was awful, wasn't it? Thanks for jumping in and helping me. I was really scared there at first, and I kind of freaked out— but I know you didn't do it on purpose. You helped go after the information we needed to deal with the problem, and I appreciate that."

This kind of modest affirmation brings stability to a child who was feeling wretched about himself. It assures him that life will go on after all. Although he caused a big-time mess, his place in the family is still intact. The sun will rise again tomorrow morning. He is not quite the outcast he was thinking he had become an hour or two before.

Hard to Do

It's hard to keep the four resolves in the middle of a disaster. Everything within us wants to blow our stack. We feel entitled to let loose our rage for just ten minutes. And perhaps, the outburst is justified. But the effect can be tragic.

I was teaching on this subject one evening in a Love-to-Nurture class at our agency when a fiftyish man volunteered a poignant illustration. He recalled the day back in Germany as a ten-year-old boy when, while playing with a chemistry set in his bedroom, he accidentally caused an explosion. The whole room erupted in flames. He ran in terror for the doorway.

He couldn't see; the chemicals had blown up directly into his face. He banged into walls, screaming in pain from the burns. Eventually he fumbled his way outside to the street, still panicked and disoriented.

Just then his mother came running out from another part of the house. What were the first words out of her mouth? "Wolfgang, you've ruined your pants!" All other issues took second place to the fact that the boy had damaged his clothing.

At this point in telling the story, the man in my class began to sob. Forty years had now passed; his injuries had healed (including his eyesight), he had immigrated to America, he had built a solid livelihood, he and his wife were now in training to be foster parents—but the sting was still there. "I felt totally, completely worthless that day," he recalled. "I can still hear her scolding me, 'Your body we can fix, but the clothes are a waste forever!'"

The need to show love regardless of the provocation is essential. Nothing good will emerge without that foundation. Children tend to think in absolutes. If they feel unloved, they assume all of life is in shambles.

This is why we have such a problem in our society with teen suicide. If kids think their parents don't care about them anymore, then what's the point of going on living? Even their romantic lives are vulnerable. If a boyfriend or girlfriend dumps them, they are absolutely devastated. They are sure no one in the whole world will ever love them again the rest of their lives.

In response, they react suddenly. They grab a gun and blow their brains out. It's faster than swallowing pills or slashing their wrists. (This is one reason for keeping weapons locked away from teenagers. Studies have shown that suicides in these homes are far less frequent.) If they had just waited thirty minutes, their despair would have slackened. But kids are not wired that way.

It is part of our responsibility as adults to keep them from moving to the edge of that cliff. I have counseled far too many parents in agony who have moaned, "If only I had been there to tell her it wasn't *that* big a deal. She didn't need to take her life. Yes, I was angry with her—but this problem could have been fixed. If only . . ."

We adults know that when we get into a fight with a family member—a sibling, our spouse, a parent—there's an underlying sense of unconditional acceptance. Yes, I'm really mad at you, but that doesn't mean I've stopped loving you. We're still in the same family. Five years from now, I'll still be at your birthday party. Ten years from now, I'll still be watching your kids grow up. None of that is threatened, even though I'm steamed at you right now.

Kids, on the other hand, don't carry this assumption. They can honestly think, *My parents no longer love me. I'm rejected. I might as well get out of here forever.* The STAR paradigm serves a vital role in preventing this kind of overreaction. When we show love regardless of the offense and proceed to work with the realities that will shape the future, the child's doomsday mentality is pushed aside.

The advice of the apostle Paul is appropriate in this context: "Bear with each other and forgive whatever grievances you may have against one another. Forgive as the Lord forgave you" (Col. 3:13). If the heavenly Father can show love toward us in every situation, we can find a way to forgive someone who wrecks the carpet. The day is probably not too far off when we'll need forgiveness ourselves.

Facing the Worst

Is this feasible when the roof truly does fall in on our heads? How would the STAR approach work in our worst nightmare with a child? What if, for example, your fifteen-year-old daughter comes into your room late one evening, leans against the closet door, gives a big sigh, and then announces, "Mom—I'm pregnant"?

Your heart will begin to race. Your knees will go weak. The room may even start to spin temporarily. You can't stop any of these reactions from happening. You're terribly upset.

But then you suck in a big breath. Maybe two of them. Inside, you ask yourself the first question, which is *How in the world am I going to show this kid that I still love her?* After all, you know she's scared. You recognize that it took a lot of courage to come in here.

Go ahead and put that into words. Wrap your arms around your daughter and say, "It must have been really hard for you to come tell me this. I love you, honey. . . . I'm in shock, but—you know, whatever we face in our family, we stick together. We're the Wilsons, and we don't bail out on each other. I'm here for you."

By now you'll both probably be crying, which is OK. Let her melt down for a few minutes. Let her sense that she still has at least one friend in the world.

Soon you can inquire about her physical well-being. "Are you feeling OK? Can I help you with anything?" Yes, you'd rather ask other, more probing questions. But there will be plenty of time for those later. This problem is not going to go away. Here at the start, your goal is to convey a tone of "I love you and care about you" instead of "I'm going to kill you" (or kill the boyfriend).

The second STAR resolve says *I will work with my child toward the ends that we select together.* This means drying your tears and gradually coming around to such queries as: "So what are we going to do about this? Have you thought it through? Where do we go from here?" The answers you get may be impractical or far-fetched. Or there may be nothing more than "I don't know." What counts is that the dialogue is underway.

The worst thing a parent can do in this moment is to start dictating: "Well, here's what you're going to do. We're going to send you to Aunt May's house in Delaware until you have the baby, so no one here will know." Or, "You're never going to see that blankety-blank Jonathan again as long as you live!" Or some other unilateral edict.

The need of the hour, instead, is *goal agreement.*

In fact, teleology is bigger than just settling on a tactic or strategy. It is about understanding the nature of the other human being. It is believing, even in this dark hour, that your daughter has a destiny on this earth. She has special qualities and talents that were given to her for a reason. Though she and her boyfriend have temporarily derailed her best future, all is not lost. The essence of who she is remains, and her parents must continue to be wise stewards of that essence.

> Your goal is to convey a tone of "I love you and care about you" instead of "I'm going to kill you."

If ever there was a time for the wisdom of "empower, don't overpower," it is this. Your daughter is in a tough predicament; how are you going to empower her? How much can you consign to her to be handled alone? What aspects require collaboration? In what ways can the next eight or nine months bring about a more mature, thoughtful, wiser young person?

Girls this age are infamous for declaring right away, "I want to keep the baby." They see it as entering a whole new chapter of life, a more adult chapter. They vaguely know that money will be a shortage for them, as well as time flexibility. But they assume "it will all work out" somehow. The adoption alternative is all too often brushed aside as too painful or even a form of disloyalty to the young life now growing within them. The fact that millions of married couples are eagerly waiting for this baby with open arms and well-stocked wallets is dismissed out of hand.

Sorting through the options together, without antagonism, is vital. It can even clarify moral issues in the teenager's mind that were never seriously considered before. "So what really is this life I'm now carrying? And what's my responsibility to that life?" It can also lead to a new openness for guidance—from God, from wise adults. A plan for the future eventually begins to crystallize.

Next comes the search for avenues of achievement. What are the parts and pieces of the next months? This includes everything from finding an ob-gyn to figuring out how to continue school to communicating with the baby's father and his family . . . the list goes on and on. Now, *which* of these activities can your daughter handle well by herself? What could she manage that would make her say, at the end of the day, "I did a good job on that one"? Which items would only frustrate her? Remember, she's probably feeling like a loser about now. Find some ways, however small, for her to win.

In time, you will even see value in rewarding her. No, not for getting pregnant in the middle of high school—that's for sure. But you can reward your daughter for diligent prenatal care of her body. When she eats healthy things and remembers to take her special vitamins, you can congratulate her. You can tell her that she looks nice, even though her tummy is starting to swell. On the biggest aspect of all—what to do with the baby once it arrives—you can reward her if you concur with the decision she eventually makes.

Throughout this long and stressful process, the STAR paradigm will help keep you majoring on the majors. It will prevent you from saying things you'll later regret. It will keep you and your child connected to each other, rather than alienated. It will steer you toward making the best of a bad situation.

Here is one way to evaluate your performance as a parent. Ask yourself this question: When her friends call and ask her how it is going, what will she say? You know there's a whole audience out there waiting for reports. In fact, some of them probably knew about the pregnancy before you did. They're all waiting to hear about the fall-out.

What you want to occur is for your daughter to say, "You know, I told my folks, and it was good that I did. It makes me feel a whole lot better now. I think we're going to make this work. I'm really glad I have my mom and dad. I'm going to come out stronger because of this."

A Diagnostic Tool

So far we've explored how the four resolves can guide us in episodes large and small. I have also found great help by simply using them to take stock of how a child's everyday life is going. Especially if he or she seems to be faltering in some way—if the grades are

slipping, if the attitude is turning sour, if motivation seems lagging—
I can silently review in my mind:

- *Does this kid feel loved? Is there somebody in his life who's telling him that?*
- *Is it clear what we're trying to accomplish? Is the kid on board with that goal?*
- *Are we all aware of his strengths? Are we making roads for him to achieve in line with those strengths? Or does he feel trapped?*
- *Do we have an intelligent reward system in place? And are we following through on what we promised? Is he getting encouragement for the right things?*

It is uncanny how often the blow-out will come to light as I review the four areas. Suddenly I say to myself, "So *that's* the problem! No wonder we've been hitting bumps recently."

> A STAR analysis can often pinpoint the
> problem because it deals with
> the most important factors that
> shape the personality.

I've even used this with school officials who are unhappy with one of our children in foster care. Running a school these days is a tough job in any regard, and when a student doesn't fit in, the urge to remove the problem by expelling or reassigning elsewhere can be strong. I can't count how many staff meetings I've attended where the main purpose of the gathering was to build the case against a student's ongoing attendance—or at least to spell out in no uncertain terms what behaviors would get the kid kicked out again. I've heard all about the no-tolerance policies on this, that, and the other.

I end up saying, "Now just hold on a minute. Before we put this child out on the curb, can we go through a few questions?" I then walk them through the four areas. Does this child feel at all loved in the classroom environment? Is there anybody he feels he can trust, or is he all alone there? Where should the educational system be going with this child? What is his destiny? What are the avenues to get there? Is he getting rewarded for the right things? It is amazing sometimes how the conversation opens up and gets beyond the letter of the law to what really would enable this child to stay in school. Teachers and principals, I am glad to say, have responded positively at times.

If a child is misbehaving in some other group setting—Boy Scouts, Girl Scouts, the Little League team, the Sunday school class—a STAR analysis can often pinpoint the problem because it deals with the most important factors that shape the personality.

If a child is failing in any environment, my instinct is always to examine that environment. Check out the surroundings first; blame the child last. Most of the time, the problem is the environment we have created, not the child.

I realize that is a bold statement, and a devil's advocate might say, "Well, you're avoiding personal responsibility. Kids need to take ownership for their own behavior."

The whole idea of the STAR paradigm is to *raise* or *enhance* personal responsibility. We need to create an environment in which, if the young person messes up, they can see it immediately and self-correct it. The entire concept of rewards and extinguishment makes it clear that if you do the right thing, you'll be praised, and if you do the wrong thing, negative consequences are going to come your way. Now, it's your choice—how are you going to conduct yourself in this setting?

Of course, this choice won't be grasped if the kid feels unloved. He will be so obsessed with his loneliness that he can't be objective about his behavior. Similarly, the need for a clear goal and for avenues to reach it are foundational. But once these are in place, the child starts to function as a fully empowered human being on this earth, aware that if he doesn't make good decisions, it's his problem and his alone.

In working with kids in foster care, many of whom have come out of wretched home environments, we keep pushing the concept of "You know, it may not be your fault—but it *is* your responsibility." Victimized kids now in therapy can dwell on all the bad things that have come their way in life. We say, "Yes, that happened. But now—what are you going to do about it? How will you make the future different from the past, for your own benefit as well as those around you? It's your call."

This is much different from "You'd better straighten up because I say so" or "I'm going to straighten you up myself." It is empowering the young person to choose a wiser road of their own free will. By the time they turn eighteen years old, we want them to hold all the necessary cards in their own hand. We want them to be fully responsible for themselves, able to analyze and self-regulate whenever needed. We want them under reliable and mature control.

That's the definition of a *star*.

CHAPTER

11

Don't Try This Alone

Pam Bates is a foster care agency's dream. When you spend your life looking for homes that can handle difficult or distressed children, you breathe a sigh of relief when you come across a Pam Bates. Her shoulder-length blond hair frames a face that is both kind and wise; children can tell this woman is going to be nice to them but won't be a pushover. After all, she has raised six kids of her own. Only the youngest, a fifteen-year-old daughter, is still at home. Pam is definitely no rookie.

"I'm just a mom," she says with a smile. "That's my gift. I love it."

When a neighboring county asked us to place a sister-and-brother combination with special needs, we thought of Pam. The eleven-year-old girl, Hannah, was quickly losing her eyesight due to macular degeneration. This malady, more common among the elderly, occurs when the macula (center region of the retina) begins breaking down, creating a blur in the straight-ahead field of vision. Only the edges remain clear. Hannah already had a big scar across her face from falling off her bicycle; she was now legally blind. The county approached us because our city happens to have the state's residential deaf-and-blind school, which might be useful to the girl at some point.

Pam Bates, we knew, had in years past lost a ten-year-old special-needs daughter of her own. We asked if she was open to taking Hannah and her younger brother, Christian. Or would this be too painful a reminder for her? "No," she said, "I'd love to help them if I can."

Hannah and Christian are doing well these days at the Bates home. But even an expert like Pam can't provide everything that's needed by herself. That became apparent one day when our home supervisor stopped by for a visit. "Hannah, how are you doing?" she asked with a light-hearted tone.

"OK," the girl said wistfully. "I just wish I could watch TV with the family when they all curl up together on the couch at night."

"Hmmm, sounds good to me," said the supervisor. "Why can't you?"

"Because I can't see the screen."

"Really?"

"Yes. I have to sit up real close and off to one side, so I don't block everybody else's view. I can see best out the side anyway. But I can't lie down or anything. It's no fun!"

Before leaving that day, the supervisor pulled Pam aside to discuss what might be done. The solution, she learned, would be a big-screen television set. "But those are really expensive," Pam added. "I don't know how we'd ever come up with one."

The home supervisor and I talked about this dilemma when she returned to the office. I began thinking about asking others to help. This was a legitimate need for making Hannah feel included in the foster family. When everybody else was laughing and giggling at the Disney movie while she felt ostracized on her chair across the room, the girl was shut out from the warmth and normality we all hoped to give her.

The next day, I put together an e-mail to five hundred core donors. I told them about Hannah's situation. I boldly said we needed to pitch in for a sixty-inch television with all the supporting technology, which would run more than two thousand dollars. I appealed to people's willingness to help make a difference for this young girl.

I still remember glancing at the screen clock when I hit "Send"— it read 2:22 on Tuesday afternoon.

By noon on Wednesday, less than twenty-two hours later, I had to send out a second e-mail communicating something I'd never done in all my years of nonprofit leadership: OK, you can stop sending money now! We have all we need for this project. The pledges had literally poured in. The average gift, by the way, was only fifteen dollars; this was not a case of one or two big donations carrying the day. People all over the area stepped up to provide this piece of equipment for the Bates home.

I tell this story to illustrate the fact that even the best parents and caregivers need a helping hand from the outside occasionally. You don't have to do this all by yourself. After all, the care of children—even well-behaved ones—is a major enterprise in life. It's a far bigger task than maintaining a yard, managing a volunteer committee, earning a master's degree, or most of the other jobs we take on as adults. Add in the extra burden of children's physical or behavior problems such as we've been discussing in this book, and the load can become overwhelming. "Help!" we want to scream.

In fact, that is exactly the right word to use. Pam Bates was too polite to ask, but when we realized her need, we jumped in to respond. Every parent needs outside support from time to time, especially if they are handling difficult offspring.

When the TV had been secured, we arranged for a surprise unveiling at the Hope & Home office. We put a big red bow on the set, gathered a large crowd of staff members, donors, and other foster families, then brought Hannah into the room. "This is for you and your home!" we shouted.

She was amazed. She turned shy and didn't know what to say, even though a big smile spread across her face. Now she could watch TV at the same distance as the rest in her family, without being banished to an up-close chair.

One of the donors on hand that special day was B. E. Tillotson, an eighty-seven-year-old man who suffers from macular degeneration, too. He is a retired fighter pilot who flew thirty-one missions over Japan in World War II, then went on to a distinguished Air Force career at both the Pentagon and NORAD. His heart had been especially touched by the fund appeal. He wanted to meet this little girl.

Before the party ended that day, the two of them sat down together in a corner. Though separated by three quarters of a century in age, they found out they shared the same ophthalmologist. They talked quietly for several minutes as the rest of us watched respectfully at a distance. "This isn't going to slow you down," the old gentleman told the young girl. "You can still make it in life, just like I've done all these years."

And by the look on eleven-year-old Hannah's face, you could tell she believed every word.

We Need One Another

The support of a larger community is a key factor in staying the course for parents and guardians of difficult kids. When we've been hurt, when our teenager has insulted us, when we feel like the world is smacking us in the face, the calming words and actions of others can stabilize us. They can also give us the courage to keep going. We are constantly reminded us that we are not the only ones.

Otherwise, when our son gets kicked out of school *again*, we feel humiliated. We assume every other parent in the world is doing it right except us. In these moments, we need the voice of others to remind us that institutions tend to streamline themselves, weeding out people who don't fit.

When our child ends up going to court, we sense the unspoken opinion of many citizens, *Let the judge go ahead and lock him up! He needs to pay for what he did. He needs to learn a lesson.* I have talked with many parents who, in their exasperation, halfway agree with that opinion . . . until they realize that the court system can easily chew up a kid, to his detriment. After all, the voting public outside is calling for toughness. They want judges to bring down the "bigger hammer" we talked about in chapter 2. *Get these no-goods off the streets.*

Parents in such a spot feel torn. They want their child to feel appropriate consequences—but if they talk too openly to the district attorney, they may end up jeopardizing their child's safety and giving him a permanent record instead of the chance to start over. They desperately need the friendship of somebody who understands the difference between wise nurturance and simple punishment.

Parental support groups hold out the promise of three main benefits:

1. *A language for processing and thinking about the problems.* We might even call this a *culture.* When parents are able to interact with other parents about "making deposits into the love account" and "goal agreement" and "avenues of achievement," they clarify their own circumstances. They figure out more readily what to do next. They go home from meetings with a clearer strategy in mind.

Theory is great, but it has to be applied in real-life settings. Words in a textbook will not jump off the page and solve problems all by themselves. They have to be implemented. When we commit ourselves to an action plan, people who are undergoing the same pain as we are have the right to hold us accountable. They can ask the hard questions at next week's meeting about whether we followed through or not.

2. *A reality check on home crises.* After all the yelling subsides and all the doors have been slammed, it's good to go for a walk with your spouse or another friend and talk about what just happened. At first, you may defend everything you did. But then, your emotions will settle down, and you can hear another person's take on the facts. You may even end up laughing at some of the absurdities.

If you want to get extra-brave, join a combination parent-teen group. Some of the most productive groups I have ever led have been those that included parents and their kids in the same circle. For one thing, participants talk much more honestly because they know that any self-serving "smoke" will quickly be blown away by the other family members present. In the presence of others, the pressure to get beyond accusations and embrace solutions is especially strong.

3. For those who believe in the value of such a thing, there is a third potential benefit: *praying together.* Our agency works with foster parents from various faiths or no faith at all, and we are careful to respect individual positions. We do find, however, that people who view their work as a calling can glean both encouragement and fresh insight by praying with others of like mind about the challenges they face.

We advise all our foster parents in advance that every support group meeting will be opened with prayer. We don't want them to be taken by surprise. So far, no one has objected.

We also have a tradition in our agency that every event of any kind—support group, board meeting, fund-raiser, staff meeting—will include an empty chair (often tipped up against the table), reserved "for the child in distress whom we haven't found yet." We pray aloud for this unknown child in our community, that we will soon be able to alleviate his or her pain.

The power of a caring community must not be minimized. My wife and I feel this strongly, perhaps because of our Native American heritage. The tribal culture has always been extremely inclusive. Children use the words *aunt* and *uncle* freely about any adult they trust, regardless of blood relationship. It is not unusual to go into an Indian home and find children from various progeny being cared for together. Similarly, adults lean on one another for wisdom and practical help in nurturing the children of the tribe. There is not the sense of "my home, my castle, and everybody else stay out of my business" that one often feels in the majority culture.

This is why the mass removal of Indian children from their culture in days past was especially disturbing. Prior to 1978, when the Indian Child Welfare Act (ICWA) became law, as many as 75 percent of our children had been taken away to boarding schools or other non-Indian settings. They suffered the loss not only of parents but of their sense of tribe as well. The traditional inclusion was shattered.

Such children have come to be known as "split feathers"—separated from the community to which they belong. We are working these days to place Indian children in Indian homes whenever possible. If we can't make that work for a given child, we still work hard to maintain cultural links by teaching Indian music, dance, art, and cooking, and the non-Indian foster parents are glad to accommodate.

Practical Recommendations

Some of the things that make support groups especially productive, we have found, are these:

1. Homogeneous membership. It works better if the parents of preschoolers cluster together, the parents of elementary age kids, and so forth. While diversity can have some benefits, more often the parents of a four-year-old will simply tune out when the parents of a seventeen-year-old start expounding on his smoking problem. The developmental stages that we studied in chapter 4 of this book do make a real difference.

2. *More than just war stories.* If the evening is consumed with lengthy tales of "My kid did this horrible thing," followed by "Well, I can top that—listen to this one," people will simply go home depressed. Group members must move on to reframing one another's perspectives, looking at the situation with fresh eyes. How might this situation be viewed *relationally* instead of *confrontationally*? The diagnostic tools of chapter 10 (STAR) are especially helpful here. Is this child feeling unloved? What are the goals that have been selected together, or have they? What new avenues of achievement might be explored? This kind of dialogue is beneficial.

3. *A leader who understands the model.* Group members can sometimes get lost in the details, rambling on and on. The leader has to corral the discussion back to what will make a difference in the child's future. It is not mandatory that leaders have lived through the pain of raising an out-of-control child themselves, although that is always helpful. What is essential is a grasp of the philosophy that turns a child from chaos to self-regulation.

4. *Comfortable schedule and surroundings.* We have found over the years that after a group has completed the foundational training, they can do well on a once-a-month frequency. These are busy people; if they have the chance to interact with each other every thirty days, that is usually suitable. The environment can be anywhere, of course, but a potluck in someone's home is among the best options. This offers adequate space for child care while the adults are talking in the other room.

The Bigger View

The work that parents and other adults do with difficult kids resides in the midst of a context even larger than the local community. We are building, for better or worse, the next generation of Americans. Our nation will be in their hands in another thirty years. On an even grander scale, the challenges of our world will be theirs to manage. These are children whom God has given us to develop; can you think of anything more strategic? He has put the future of the human race in our hands.

I remember as a sixteen-year-old kid sitting with my girlfriend in a little church listening to a young minister read the parable of the workers in the vineyard (Matt. 20:1–16). This is the story Jesus told about a grape grower who went to the day-labor market early in the morning and hired a crew to work for one denarius (the normal day's pay in that era). Not having enough workers for the task at hand, he went back a couple of hours later and hired more, promising, "I will pay you whatever is right."

He was back again at noon, at three in the afternoon, and even at five o'clock, adding to his crew. Then came payday as the sun was setting. The vineyard owner shocked them by paying *everybody* one denarius—which set off a howl of protest from the all-day workers.

The vineyard owner replied that he had kept his word to everyone; no one had been cheated. Meanwhile, he had a right to be generous or even extravagant with his own money if he felt like it. The closing line of the story from Jesus: "So the last will be first, and the first will be last."

The young minister in the church that day asked, "What is this parable trying to teach us? Yes, I know the standard interpretation: that those who follow Christ from the beginning of their years and those who start their spiritual walk much later all wind up with the same reward—heaven. That's what most of us have been taught about this story.

> We are building, for better or worse,
> the next generation of Americans.
> Our nation will be in their hands
> in another thirty years.

"But I'd like to throw out a new idea today. I don't discount the traditional view. It's valid. I see something additional in this parable, however. I see that in order to get the job done, *God needs us all.* Every single soul is valuable to Him. Everybody has a role to play."

The poor misshapen baby who comes into the world with dreadful birth defects, suffers in agony for three minutes, and dies in the delivery room—that soul is just as important to God as the person who lives a hundred years and has monuments built to his name all over the country. The brilliant, the disabled, the gorgeous, the homely, and everyone in between have a place in the divine economy.

In my present work, that parable has become my favorite Scripture passage. I tell anxious parents, "It's not really about whether your kid is turning out better or worse than somebody else's kid, you know. You have a covenant relationship with that child, and you're giving it your best shot. That is all God expects.

"And I'm here to help you make this work. You and I are in this together. Guess what—you *will* get to the end of the day. And you will get what's fair to you."

We too often think God will judge us someday according to our successes on this earth, or lack thereof. "He who dies with the most outstanding kids wins." We use words such as "Yes, Tyler's been accepted to Harvard; we're really blessed." The implication is that if Tyler had been turned away by even the local community college, your family would have been cursed. God would be frowning at you, along with the rest of humanity.

How many parents are tormenting themselves wondering, "Why can't my child be like those kids on the honor roll? I've done such a terrible job of parenting." A variation of this theme in some families is "Why couldn't you be more like your brother down the hallway? He never gives us a minute's trouble."

God created every child unique. Every person counts equally. The thirteen-year-old who is a total brat is absolutely loved by God in the same measure as the future valedictorian who sits next to him in algebra class. Yes, he gets dreadfully out of line, and part of that is his responsibility. But another part of the responsibility belongs to us adults to find things he can do well. God is asking us to move such children into paths that lead upward instead of in the direction of dead ends.

Will we succeed at this? Maybe, maybe not. We can only try—and stop judging ourselves. The master of the vineyard asks for no more than that.

We live in such a competitive world. We assume we're like the football coach who, if he experiences a 3–11 season, knows it will be only a matter of weeks until the school superintendent, college president, or owner of the team calls him in for a talk. "Sorry, pal—we need a 'different style of leadership' for next season," he says. "You're done here." Parents often feel they're being rated by how their kids perform on the gridiron of life. What does the scoreboard say? Am I doing well enough at least to keep from getting booed?

God doesn't rate parents that way, and neither should we. To such a mentality I say, *Tear down the scoreboard! Tear down the scoreboard!* Stop comparing your child to the kid next door or the standard you read in a book or magazine somewhere. Turn your attention instead to the purpose God intended for this individual boy or girl, and focus your energy on bringing that purpose to maturity.

In one class where I was teaching this topic, a woman started to cry. "I just realized something," she admitted. "My daughter made a comment the other day that really surprised me." We all knew that her eight-year-old girl was developmentally delayed "She had been giving me trouble about going down to visit my sister and her kids. 'You're a mean mom to me there,' my daughter said.

"I denied it. But now that I think about it, I guess I just get all uptight when we walk into that house. Her kids—my daughter's cousins—are all high achievers; they're in the gifted and talented programs at school; their 'A' papers are all over the refrigerator. And I feel bad about my child by comparison. I guess it shows in the way I relate to her. She can feel the tension."

We agreed with her insight. By the end of the discussion, the mother said, "Next time we go for a visit, I'm going to take some of my daughter's artwork to show. I want her to sense that I love her and am proud of her just the way she is."

Whether your relatives and neighbors think you're a winner or not is beside the point. Sometimes the last truly can become the first.

Don't Give Up Too Soon

You may not know the results of your labor for a long time. Payday for parents comes at unpredictable intervals. There's no promise that when the child reaches age eighteen or twenty-one, all the issues will be resolved and a healthy adulthood can proceed— even though that's certainly our goal. Sometimes the fruit of our work is delayed for years.

I will never forget a foster family, the Johnsons, who took in a "wild child" by the name of Mona. She was fresh out of the psychiatric treatment center where I worked at the time. Mona was, you might say, too physically endowed for her own good. Older boys had flocked around her, pulling her into the world of sex and drugs, until she had dropped out of school. She had attempted suicide, which led to the residential placement for her. Our professional staff diagnosed her with borderline personality disorder and another problem called oppositional defiant disorder. (The first of these is an overwhelming sense of emptiness that results in self-destructive behavior; the second is an antisocial "rebel without a cause" attitude of constant defiance and opposition to all structure. Mona was a toxic combination of both.) Our therapists had tried their best to address these problems, and we all hoped she would continue to improve.

Now she arrived on the Johnson doorstep and lasted all of one week. Within those seven days, she brought drugs into the house, stole household items to sell on the street, sneaked a boy into her bedroom to have sex, broke every curfew she was given, and finally ran away. The Johnsons understandably reached for the aspirin bottle and said good riddance. I thanked them for at least trying to help Mona. We all assumed we had failed.

Some five years later she showed up in my office, now twenty years old. She was covered in tattoos and frankly admitted to me that she was working as a stripper in Omaha. I could tell by her appearance that she was still on drugs. She wanted to see her old psychiatrist, she said.

"Yes, Mona, I can help you with that," I replied. I set up an appointment for a few days later. She said thanks and then never showed up.

Another four years passed. Suddenly, there was Mona again! She looked a little more stabilized by now. "How are you doing!" I said with excitement. "It's good to see you."

"Well, I'm not stripping anymore, if that's what you mean," she replied. "I had a baby. But I couldn't take care of it, so they took it away from me. I don't know where it is now. . . . Um, I need a place to live. Got any ideas?"

"Tell me how it's going with your medications," I said, changing the subject.

"Oh, I don't do that anymore," she admitted. "Got other stuff to keep me going, if you know what I mean. . . ."

I gave her directions to a homeless shelter that I thought would be safe for her, and I urged her to think again about getting back on her meds. With that, she vanished for the second time.

Once or twice thereafter, she came back through Colorado and gave me a call. I kept trying to keep the connection alive, hoping I could still help her get her act together at this late stage. I didn't see any real progress, however.

Then one day Mona showed up again, now thirty-two years old. Her hair was pulled back in a ponytail, and she was wearing a fairly nice outfit. She looked different, even with the tattoos.

"Mona! What's up?" I said, standing up to greet her.

> Mona and her friend stepped out onto the
> sidewalk and tried to figure out what part
> of town they were in. . . .

"Well, I thought I'd stop by again," she began. "Several things have changed for me." She began telling me the saga of a big fight with her live-in boyfriend that had turned violent. She decided to leave Omaha that night and headed west 150 miles to Grand Island, Nebraska, where a girl she had worked with at the strip club now lived.

"We got all dressed up that first Saturday night and headed out to a bar," Mona admitted. "A bunch of guys were there, of course, and by the end of the evening they wanted us to come over to this one apartment. At that point, we were too smashed to know better, so we went."

The rest of the night was a miasma of more drinking, sex, and cocaine. The next morning, Mona and her friend stepped out onto the sidewalk and tried to figure out what part of town they were in. They began walking, trying to find their way home, when they came upon a church with a sign out front: "Free Pancake Breakfast—Everyone Welcome."

They looked at each other, still in their short skirts, tight tops, and high heels from the night before, and snickered. "Hey, since we don't have any money, let's go in here and get some food!" one said to the other. "We'll totally freak them out." In the door they walked.

To their amazement, people welcomed them. Nobody said a word about their provocative attire. They were pleasantly served a hearty breakfast, and when they sat down at a table to eat, several church folk came over to talk with them. No one frowned or went whispering to the minister that the two maybe ought to be asked to leave.

"Somehow in the conversation, we gave them my girlfriend's phone number," Mona continued. "A day or two later, somebody actually called us to say, 'Hey, it was good to meet you. Come on back next Sunday morning for another pancake breakfast! We do this every week. We'd love to have you stop by.' These people actually wanted us.

"So we kept going. I'm still there, in fact. That's what has given me a whole new direction for my life. I'm a Christian now.

"I met this really cute guy at church, an electrician. He's a Christian too. In fact, we're engaged! We're going to be married in a few months."

"Wow, Mona, that's incredible!" I said.

"And when we set up our house," she continued, "I know how I want it to look. I've been thinking how cool it would be to have a fireplace in the living room, with two wingback chairs on either side, and then there'll be a leather couch facing from the other side of the room. And in the bedroom, I want to have the curtains that . . ." She talked on and on in great detail. She described her dream kitchen. She told me colors and patterns and furnishings that would make up her home.

I sat there stunned, as it gradually dawned on me she was describing the Johnson home to a T. That house she had terrorized so long ago was still in her memory bank, despite all the intervening years of craziness. To her, it represented the way a real home with a real family ought to be. Now at last, Mona wanted one just like it for herself and her groom. I choked back the tears just thinking about it.

I desperately wanted to tell the Johnsons what I had heard but had no way to get in touch with them. All contact had been lost. They'll never know how the seed they planted in that rebellious teenager during just seven days eventually bore fruit. Their parenting was not a failure after all. What they thought was a disaster turned out for good in the end.

We may never know until eternity the results of our labor with difficult kids. As Mother Teresa famously put it, "God did not call me to be successful but to be faithful." We give our best to stabilizing those who seem out of control, working and planning and collaborating and praying with all our might. And for every positive result we are privileged to see, we give thanks. This is still the greatest job in the world.

NOTES

Chapter 1

1. Wyoming Department of Education, "2003 Wyoming Youth Risk Behavior Study."

2. The Alan Guttmacher Institute, "Facts in Brief: Teen Sex and Pregnancy" (New York, 1996).

3. Centers for Disease Control and Prevention, "Youth Risk Behavior Surveillance—United States, 2001."

Chapter 2

1. Marilyn Elias, "Electronic world swallows up kids' time, study finds," *USA Today*, 9 March 2005.

Chapter 7

1. Antoine de Saint-Exupéry, *The Little Prince*, English translation by Katherine Woods (San Diego: Harcourt Brace & Co., 1943), 68.

2. Ibid., 70.

Chapter 9

1. Alfie Kohn, *Punished by Rewards* (Boston: Houghton Mifflin, 1993, 1999).

A FREE Study Guide to this book is available for groups as well as individuals.
- Eleven sessions, approximately one hour each
- Worksheets and handouts included

Download from the Publisher's Web site at:
www.KidsInCrisisBook.com